Rewire Your Brain

2 in 1

How To Control Your Thoughts To Stop Overthinking, Anxiety and Worry

Jennifer Ferguson

Copyright 2019 © Jennifer Ferguson

All rights reserved.

No part of this guide may be reproduced in any form without permission in writing from the publisher except in the case of review.

Legal & Disclaimer

The following document is reproduced below with the goal of providing information that is as accurate and reliable as possible.

This declaration is deemed fair and valid by both the American Bar Association and the Committee of Publishers Association and is legally binding throughout the United States.

Furthermore, the transmission, duplication or reproduction of any of the following work including specific information will be considered an illegal act irrespective of if it is done electronically or in print. This extends to creating a secondary or tertiary copy of the work or a recorded copy and is only allowed with an express written consent from the Publisher. All additional right reserved.

The information in the following pages is broadly considered to be a truthful and accurate account of facts, and as such any inattention, use or misuse of the information in question by the reader will render any resulting actions solely under their purview. There are no scenarios in which the publisher or the original author of this work can be in any fashion deemed liable for any hardship or damages that may befall them after undertaking information described herein.

Additionally, the information in the following pages is intended only for informational purposes and should thus be thought of as universal. As befitting its nature, it is presented without assurance regarding its prolonged validity or interim quality. Trademarks that are mentioned are done without written consent and can in no way be considered an endorsement from the trademark holder.

Table of Contents

Book 1: Rewire Your Mind 7

Introduction 8

Chapter 1: Becoming Lucid 19

Chapter 2: Secrets Of The Mind You Need To Know 34

Chapter 3: The Most Complicated Object In The Known Universe 84

Chapter 4: The Body - The Unconscious Mind? 104

Chapter 5: The Expansive Environment 142

Chapter 6: Illness and Wellness 151

Chapter 7: How To Improve Brain Health With Meditation 189

Conclusion 219

Book 2: Mind Hacking 226

Introduction 227

Chapter 1: What Is Mind Hacking? 236

Chapter 2: Emotion and Your Brain 251

Chapter 3: How Emotion Translates to Behavior: The Good, the Bad and the Ugly 271

Chapter 4: Neuroplasticity and the Science Behind Forming Habits 294

Chapter 5: Letting Go of Worry, Overthinking, and Anxiety 313

Chapter 6: Mind Hacking Step 1: Identify Negative Influences and Habits 333

Chapter 7: Mind Hacking Step 2: Set Your Goals and Learn to Visualize 352

Chapter 8: Mind Hacking Step 3: One Step at a Time 372

Chapter 9: Meditation Techniques 392

Chapter 10: Moving Forward: 10 Daily Practices to Strengthen Self-Confidence 412

Conclusion 434

Book 1:
Rewire Your Mind

How To Change Your Mind To Live A Successful And Positive Life On Your Own Terms

Introduction

Have you ever been sleeping and dreaming a super intense and realistic dream, and suddenly in the dream you "awaken" and you realize that you are dreaming?

It's an exhilarating realization, understanding in that moment that you have the opportunity to experience the reality of your choosing - but it's fleeting. It's difficult to maintain the awakened state without leaving the dream, and you have to really focus at first to maintain your awareness. If you get good at it, through purposeful practice and repetition, you can maintain the awakened state while also allowing your mind to "reach out," if you will, as though you have one foot firmly rooted in the now, while the other is free to further engineer the events of the dream. Once you can maintain the balance of your awareness, you can remain awake as you continue to dream.

Perhaps the first time you awaken in a dream, the most you get out of it is the awareness of having woken, but then you quickly go back "under," or, upon waking in the dream, you also wake from the sleep and it's over. With practice, however, you eventually become able to maintain the awareness of being awake in the dream, while staying in the dream, and you are able to react to events with a new awareness (if it's a bad dream, you may leave the situation, or alter your reaction to it, etc.... if it's a good dream, relax and enjoy it ;). As you progress, you may find yourself better able to extend the "now" moment and stay awake and aware in the dream long enough to actually begin to engineer it and to do what you most want. Synthesize your process with your awareness in waking life, and you can extend and enhance your experience all the more.

However that may apply to your dreaming experience, returning to the present via your conscious awareness and your senses help to maintain an overall balance as far as staying "awake" within your dream, and the more that you practice being lucid, the more expansive your awareness becomes.

You can engineer your dream reality and map your journey, remaining flexible to all that comes your way by simply allowing, accepting, and adapting, because in your awakened state you know that you have the ultimate weapon: choice. Your dream is yours to shape. Do you dare to believe? If so, you must be wholly accountable for yourself. You can't be both victim and master of your destiny. You must choose which path to take – victim or master, and that doesn't mean that you won't encounter situations beyond your control, but your reaction to those situations, your perceptions, and the way in which you adapt shapes your reality, your present moment, and your future.

We also now know that the events of a dream, to the brain, aren't overly different than the events of real life – your body is just temporarily paralyzed during sleep to keep you from acting out your dreams.

So what if you could do this in real life? What if you could "awaken" within the dream of your life, of your reality, and of your perception of your reality, and take the wheel? You control your reality by being the master of your thoughts, your words, your emotions, your beliefs, your intentions, your actions, and your choices.

Waking life isn't for the faint of heart. It also

requires that you take responsibility for who you are, how you think, how you act, where you are in life, where you want to go, what you can achieve, and what you believe about your self-worth. What do you EXPECT your future to look like? What do you BELIEVE about yourself and about your ability to achieve your deepest desires? What do you believe about your deepest desires? Do you have the COURAGE to honor the desires that are closest to your heart? Do you know what those are?

Resist nothing that comes your way. A ship can't just float along, perceiving itself a victim of the river. It must sail with intention. And that doesn't mean that storms won't happen, but as a vessel you must navigate THROUGH them with clear and courageous purpose, understanding that storms are a part of life. Some are unfair because we live in a world that has lost its balance. Absurdities and atrocities happen daily, everywhere, and have for centuries. Suffering never goes away, but we can learn how to adapt, how to change, and how to survive and thrive despite life's circumstances. Theories evolve and adapt and change every day, and truths that we hold as groups of people and as individuals change as new ways of thinking emerge. How can we ever know what is true? Western medicine has only recently discovered an organ that it hadn't previously encountered, neuroscience is in the infancy of beginning to understand that the brain is inherently plastic, and the space community is discovering new planets daily. The impossible becomes increasingly possible every day, with new frontiers yet to explore. Individuals and groups are awakening and dismantling systems within themselves, in their communities, and around the world, and more and more people are rising up to meet the challenges, consequences, and dreams of the future.

As a master of your vessel, you have a destination and you are on course, ready to bend, adapt, and allow whatever comes your way, because what other choice do you have? You can't control the river, but to allow, and to flow WITH circumstances is to choose the path of least resistance, and in doing so you begin to understand that though there are many destinations, the truest destination is the journey itself. Does allowing mean condoning or silence? Of course not, but within the realm of your own mind, you can calm your own waters and make bold and enlivened moves with confidence and courage. "Right now" is the ultimate destination, and awakening to that "now" is the key to becoming the master of your world within. We obviously share the world with many people, and so it's easy to debate notions of thoughts creating reality when there are so many thoughts happening everywhere all the time. But how CAN you use your thoughts to shape your reality?

What if you are already where you need to be, with all of the necessary tools already in your arsenal? What if all that you conceive of exists, and you just have to head down to the proverbial post office to pick up your package. Do you believe that it's there waiting for you? Do you believe that you are worthy? Dare you make the journey? As they say, all journeys contain a destination that is unknown to the traveler...

You never know, maybe you set out on a journey toward one dream, and end up meeting a dream along the way that you couldn't have yet fathomed; something better than anything you could have dreamed until that point. Perhaps on your journey, you slay personal demons and you fight battles in the battlefields of thought. Perhaps you brave shipwrecks, endure heartache, survive the odds, and pull swords from stone. You conquer dragons, earn your wings, walk the darkness of your underworld, and unearth your holy grail. Perhaps you make the voyage, only to reach your destination and find that the journey WAS the destination. Perhaps the ultimate destiny is that of the phoenix – the ultimate transformation; the alchemists gold.

You must make the voyage to find out.

The concept of manifestation is to consciously and intentionally shape your personal reality through your thoughts, your beliefs, your actions, your expectations, and your emotional detachment to the outcome. How do you know whether or not some unforeseen or uncontrollable circumstance is a fortune or a misfortune? Your perception will become the truth. Remaining unattached to the outcome, emotionally, allows for peace of mind, smooth sailing, and greater efficiency. When you are in a state of allowing, or essentially, the state of unattachment, you are "going with the flow," if you will, and you are therefore moving more efficiently toward your desired destination. Does this mean that you do not experience emotion? Does this mean that you condone unfair circumstances, or that you sit passively by while life happens? No! However, what this does mean, is that in every moment you are able to return to yourself to regain your personal balance, and in doing so, you let go of what you can't control and allow the now to be what it is, including your own reactions to that now. Feel the emotions that you feel, allow your truest reactions, and observe them, embrace them, and shape them as it serves you. If you are angry, does it serve you to pretend that you aren't? If you aren't releasing your emotions... where are they going? Allowing also means allowing whatever is going on in your inner world to be where it is and when it is without judgment. How can you air out a closet if you don't open the door? Trust in your journey, and trust in yourself as the architect of your destiny. Build your ship, chart your path, know the waters, and manifest.

Throughout the course of this book we will navigate the waters of the mind, the brain and the body, illness and wellness, environment, perception, reality, intention, action, and the ways in which we can live our lives on our own terms, taking into account the importance of thoughts, words, belief systems, culture, environment, biology, choice, action, and privilege, and how these factors affect the process of changing your mind.

Chapter 1: Becoming Lucid

EVOLUTION

If we want to change our minds as individuals, we must also understand our minds within the context of history, of culture, of economic class, of privilege, and ultimately within the context of the planet. As we evolve as a species, we must think bigger and in terms of our planet more than ever before. What is evolution in the 21st century? Perhaps it is - for it must be, the evolution of consciousness; the evolution of thought, intention, and action in service of the global collective, and the undoing of the systems of the past.

If you rouse yourself from your programming and you awaken to the reality of your life, your dreams, your longing, and also your responsibilities with regard to where you are on the ship that is this planet, society, culture, etc., and you succeed in changing your mind in a holistic way (in such a way that it benefits not only you but society at large), you become responsible for the application of your new knowledge to the way you live your life. Once you awaken within the dream, you must take the wheel in as many ways as you possibly can. The little things add up, and some of the littlest things are conscious thoughts, beliefs, words, and the ways in which we interact with and view ourselves.

"Until you make the unconscious conscious, it will direct your life and you will call it fate." – Carl Jung

Have you ever noticed synchronistic symbols or numbers in your life? Repeated themes, repeated dreams or recurrent situations? Repeating patterns in relationships, cycles of behavior, or themes that re-appear throughout your life? These are the details of your waking dream – the content of your unconscious mind. According to dream expert Beverly D'Urso, the trick to becoming more lucid in your dreams is to pay attention to the details. Macrocosmically, becoming lucid and expanding your awareness in waking life is also about paying attention to the details – the details that are everywhere within your lifestyle, your daily habits, your thoughts, your dreams, your beliefs, and your reality. Why do you do what you do?

THE ART OF AWARENESS

There is a notion in Yaqui thought regarding the idea of "stalking" oneself, or essentially, "watching" or observing one's behavior as it happens. It's a far more extensive concept than we have time to visit in this book, but essentially, it's about observing your reactions. Observe your habitual thoughts and routines. Observe your moods, and if your moods shift, observe what triggered that shift. Observe your dreams, and observe the symbols of your dreams. The unconscious is both literal, and metaphorical, and it works in images – think in terms of words, language, and symbols – what programs are running beneath the surface?

Lucidity, awareness, and the return to the present keeps you balanced at the wheel of your life. When you are driving a vehicle, most of it is muscle memory, because you'd repeated the action with attention and intent so often that you had coded it into your unconscious mind and body. Regardless, whenever you operate a vehicle, you must be in the present moment, correct? You must be ever-aware of what is going on. So are you the driver or the passenger in your life? Are you asleep in the backseat? Are you asleep at the wheel? What does it take to effectively take the wheel of your life with awareness and intent?

Once you wake up, take the wheel, and practice the art of awareness, you can shift gears, raise your vibration, hit the fast lane, and explore the highest highways. Perhaps you prefer the back roads and the countryside, or you'd like to park the car and walk. Either way, directing your attention back to the present moment puts you back in the driver's seat.

CLEANING THE LINK

So basically, in order to align with the great "Intent," "Spirit," "God," "Universe, "Higher Self," the one that watches the watcher, the greater "You," you must first master your awareness and clean your connecting link. What does that mean for you?

Whatever it means for you, cleaning any sort of abstract "connection to source" would seem to require the cleaning of the spirit via the journey to the bottom of the well of the soul to explore the contents of the heart, to expose the roots of the weeds, to unearth ones deepest wounds, and to bring those treasures to the light. It's the hero's journey – the archetypal dark night of the soul, the odyssey, the quest to the phoenix; the journey from caterpillar to butterfly. That journey may take a lifetime, a moment, a day, or it may be a specific event or trauma, but whatever it is, you know it once the dawn arrives and you can look back at your journey in the glory of its light. The way through the labyrinth is to trust your intuition, to act on that trust, to let go of attachment to outcome, and to understand that the destination IS journey. If you are able to be alone with yourself, wherever you find yourself, and calm your own storm, you have achieved a milestone in the quest to master your mind. Life has many destinations and many journeys. It has many storms, heartaches, and tragedies, and the point isn't to eliminate any of these things, or to find the best way to avoid them, the point is to learn how to navigate them, so that wherever you find yourself, you can be there fully, without being capsized by the anxieties of tomorrow or the sorrows of yesterday. Be in them, be with them, embrace them, but do it on your terms rather than becoming a victim of the waves of your own emotions. The journey is an experiential way of learning some of life's most esoteric lessons because no one can take your journey but you. The treasures and the secrets hidden within your journey are yours and yours alone. No one but you can unearth them, and only you can carry them to the light.

Upon your return from the journey, transformed from ash to phoenix and armed with your flowered wounds and treasures alchemized from tragedy, you exist within a new awareness, possessing the ability to manipulate that awareness at will, because you have conquered the depths of your own Hades and risen to a new awareness of what is possible. From the vantage point of this new awareness, you are now better able to operate from the driver's seat of your vessel and manipulate the contents of your reality.

Become your own partner first before you seek without. Be your own best friend, the person you come home to every night whether you come home to someone or not. Practice self-care in the same way that you would care for a partner, and honor your needs without anger or shame. Stalk your reactions – all of them, and make your awareness of yourself a habit. Here's a real-life example of some every day stalking:

A woman burned her arm on an espresso machine. The scalding water shot out and burned her whole forearm, leaving a huge blister. She was a woman who was practiced in the art of stalking, and had been for some time, and observed herself reacting to the burn as it happened. She noted, almost immediately, that her reaction to the burn was one of love and care, rather than that of annoyance and burden, which was new and quite notable for her. It was a very subtle, essentially unconscious reaction on her part, but because she was actively stalking herself as a lifestyle, she caught the reaction as it happened and was able to observe it. She noted the change in her unconscious, achieved over time, through attention to self-care, self-awareness, and a conscious effort to change her unconscious perceptions regarding herself, and subsequently, the world.

The more that you engage in the details of life via the art of stalking, observation, or whatever you want to call it, the more exponential the experience becomes until it becomes habitual.

Take classical singers, for example, or yogis. The breathing that is practiced both in singing and in yoga is a style of breathing that is essentially intended. Breathing, for singers, causes the diaphragm to expand almost seven inches, whereas regular every day breathing moves the diaphragm about an inch or two. In the beginning, the breathing is a bit of a chore and takes much intent and effort, but after a while, the breathing becomes not only easier, but habitual and eventually unconscious.

If you want to code something into your unconscious, REPEAT IT.

It seems to follow that the cleaner the "connecting link," the higher the vibration, and the clearer the intuition. Your connecting link is your own, and your process, your feelings, and your triumphs are yours. Don't worry about how other people are cleaning their links, or how clean they are, or how far along they are in the process. You can't measure your connection to your own spirit or your life's progress by any other standard than your own, and the most effective cleaning is the most authentic one. Get real about the contents of your inner well. Embrace yourself and integrate yourself into the whole that you already see for your future.

"While we dream the assemblage point moves very gently and naturally. Mental balance is nothing but the fixing of the assemblage point on one spot we're accustomed to. Dreams make that point move, and dreaming is used to control that natural movement." – Don Juan

Lucid dreaming itself is an excellent exercise in practiced awareness, and in intended creation. Macrocosmically, examine the state of your life and practice the mental habits in your daily life that you want to code into your unconscious, and extend to your future. Get in the habit of taking note of the details of your everyday life. What does your day look like? How does that mirror, microcosmically, your whole life? Take your daily life, your habits, your thoughts, the foods you eat, the people you interact with, the things you do and use it as a micro-blueprint for your life as a whole. Alter the little things, change the little habits, and it will snowball into your bigger picture. In the same way that the littlest steps of a practice (music, sports, etc.) are fundamental to the bigger picture (muscle memory, technique), so the details of your everyday life are fundamental to the creation and outcome of your life as a whole. How do you feel about your daily life? Do you wake up happy? Excited for the day? Fulfilled? Does your day bring you energy or does it steal your energy? What things do you enjoy about your day? What things do you not enjoy? What do you want to keep? What would you like to discard or rewire?

"Sorcerers live their lives in hours." Little steps have to happen until your stride becomes confidently longer, or you'll essentially remain in the same place ever dreaming of more. It's easy to get overwhelmed by the enormity of life and of the future, but if you return to where you are you can begin to chart your next move. You don't have to know your next ten moves, or your next destination, or how you will get there, just worry about your very next move, however minute that may be. Follow those little thoughts that prompt you out of your routine, or those serendipities that seem to show up with such coincidence. Dare to take that little leap, even with only the mind, to those crazy places in the margins of the possible. Maybe that thing that you thought was a "sign," IS a sign. Dare to trust your intuition enough to take action, yet remain balanced, keeping one foot in the reality of where you are while you consider how to get where you'd like to be.

We live in a society full of authorities. Doctors and health professionals that tell you about the health of YOUR body, experts in every field imaginable feeding us endless information on the "shoulds" and the "shouldn'ts," all the while uncovering new "truths" and banishing others. How can we know what is true and what isn't? Being true to oneself in modern society, and acting on that truth is oftentimes an act of bravery. Believe in yourself enough to believe in the leap of faith, while also being perfectly fine if you fall. Failing contains a magic that can only be reaped experientially.

Before anything can "be," it must first "be" within the realm of the conceptual. Before you can produce a sound with your voice, you must first "hear" that sound in the auditorium of your mind, and if you desire a reality that vibrates at a certain frequency, do what you can to attune to that frequency.

Chapter 2: Secrets Of The Mind You Need To Know

"The conscious mind determines the actions; the unconscious mind determines the reactions, and the reactions are just as important as the actions." ~E. Stanley Jones

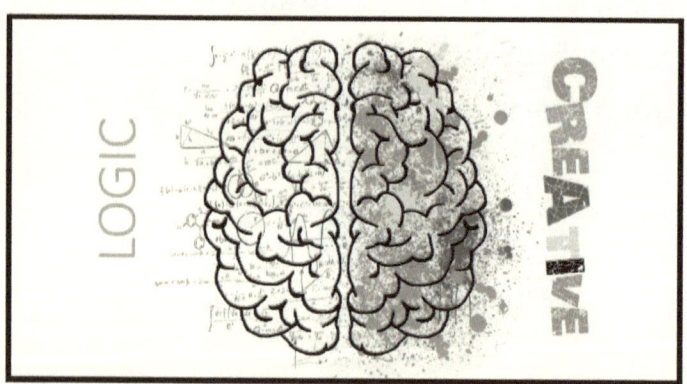

The unconscious mind plays a far larger role with regard to how we perceive reality than we may realize. Studies were conducted by Dr. John Bargh, in which participants were to meet a stranger and assess how "warm" or "cold" they perceived that person to be after having only met them for a moment. Before the subjects were introduced to the strangers, the researchers had them briefly hold a cup of either warm or iced coffee and assessed the reactions between the groups. The group that had held the warm coffee perceived the strangers to be "warmer," overall than the group that had held the cold coffee.

Why?

The unconscious is always watching, adjusting, calculating, perceiving, receiving and protecting. Much of what we consider to be conscious responses are governed largely by the unconscious mind. Have you ever been writing something while looking at something else and you accidentally write down the thing that you are looking at? By using related concepts of "warm" and "cold," researchers were able to prompt and measure an unconscious reaction to a situation across a group of people.

Were the findings also subject to the expectations of the researchers? Who can know? The mind, the brain that houses it, and the nature and contents of the universe are the greatest mysteries of science, but we are only able to observe and measure as far as our technology and tools allow. Who knows what the future of knowledge holds with regard to the power of the mind, the mysteries of the brain, and our connection to the universe around us.

All species are born into billions of years of collective memory – instincts, and human beings are no exception.... except that we have drastically changed over time, and one of our most chronic conditions as a society now, is stress. Modern stress may be a sudden fire truck siren sending your nervous system into action or a public speaking engagement, rather than a bear sighting during forest foraging or an imminent enemy. Our bodily systems are under constant attack in modern life, and stress is a chronic state for many people. When a stressful event occurs, be that an impending deadline, rush-hour traffic, or perhaps an unexpected run-in with a romantic interest, the autonomic nervous system reacts with a 'fight or flight' response. The activation of this response releases stress hormones such as cortisol and adrenaline and has rapid effects on multiple bodily systems. Heart rate and blood pressure increase, muscles tense, perspiration ensues, attention narrows, and the responses of both the digestive and immune systems are suppressed. Chronic stress also causes systemic inflammation due to the excess levels of cortisol, and cognitive functions are limited due to the narrowing of focus under duress.

Stress also adversely affects the gut due to the overflow of stress hormones that increase the permeability of the gut lining. If bacteria are detected passing through the gut wall, the immune system jumps into action, subsequently affecting the composition of the gut microbiota. A study on stress and gut bacteria in red squirrels and rat pups that had been separated from their mothers in infancy demonstrated that the greater the stress, the lower the diversity of the gut bacteria, resulting in food sensitivities, digestive issues, and an overall adverse impact on mental health.

How much is your stress worth to you?

Recent studies published by the U.S. National Library of Medicine had the following findings:

"The bidirectional communication between the central nervous system and gut microbiota, referred to as the gut-brain-axis, has been of significant interest in recent years. Increasing evidence has associated gut microbiota to both gastrointestinal and extra-gastrointestinal diseases. Dysbiosis and inflammation of the gut have been linked to causing several mental illnesses including anxiety and depression, which are prevalent in society today. Probiotics have the ability to restore normal microbial balance, and therefore have a potential role in the treatment and prevention of anxiety and depression. This review aims to discuss the development of the gut microbiota, the linkage of dysbiosis to anxiety and depression, and possible applications of probiotics to reduce symptoms. A healthy gut function has been linked to normal central nervous system (CNS) function. Hormones, neurotransmitters and immunological factors released from the gut are known to send signals to the brain either directly or via autonomic neurons.

Recently, studies have emerged focusing on variations in the microbiome and the effect on various CNS disorders, including, but not limited to anxiety, depressive disorders, schizophrenia, and autism. This review focuses on the GBA in the context of anxiety and depressive disorders. Therapeutic interventions to treat dysbiosis, or disturbance in the gut, and mitigate its effects on the GBA are only recently coming to the forefront as more is known about this unique relationship. As a result, research has been done on the use of probiotics in the treatment of anxiety and depression both as a standalone therapy and as an adjunct to commonly prescribed medications."

WAYS IN WHICH YOU CAN ALLEVIATE STRESS

- Identify the things in your life that cause both conscious and unconscious stress –

"stalk" yourself.

- Work to alleviate and balance your stress load. Obviously, things don't happen overnight, but little changes here and there in your routine will add up physically, mentally and spiritually.

- Take time for yourself – recharge in solitude, or in whatever it is that charges you – identify what brings you joy, energy, life, etc., and drink from that well often.

- Cushion your activities with time, allow your body and mind to rest, just as silence is to music – it will enliven everything else.

- Organize your priorities – where do you put your time, energy, etc.... what do you believe is most valuable? Time, rest, sleep, happiness, etc...

- ✓ Physical activity.

- ✓ Change your mind at the moment – watch a movie, go for a walk, change your mind in the moment by changing your activity and/or environment.

- ✓ Try to get enough sleep!

THOUGHTS

Returning to our discussion of the unconscious, intent, and our inherited "instincts," or memories, let's take an aside and investigate the power of words and their context within the unconscious.

Have you heard of Dr. Masaru Emoto and his water crystal experiments? Ask the internet about it. Basically, he took water and exposed it to various words, some examples include love, peace, and gratitude, and these words produced beautiful crystals once the water had been crystallized. Hateful words, as well as identities such as Adolf Hitler, produced horrid and ugly crystals. Emoto also took samples of "holy water," which produced beautiful crystals, (how did the water know it was "holy?") and water with intentions assigned to it - prayers said over it. Again, how did the water know?

Was it the expectation of the scientists?
Was it the collective memory inherent in the words and their intent and use over time?

Was it the collective assignment of meaning to the words used? How did the water know and why did it happen?

What IS collective consciousness?!

Either way, this water experiment is a testament to the effect of words on both the unconscious and conscious mind. Take negatives, for example. The unconscious is literal – if you spend your energy thinking about what you DON'T want, or what you DON'T have, your unconscious mind is going to take your thoughts literally. Perhaps you don't want to have anxiety, so rather than feeding your unconscious the idea of anxiety, ruminate rather, on what you DO want. When you are driving a car, where you direct your attention is where you end up unconsciously driving.... The more you ruminate over what you are missing, the more you essentially bathe in the energy of all that you don't have.

What about the thoughts or the beliefs that you have about yourself? How do you speak to and feel about your mainly-water self?

Words matter! Use your words to your benefit! Speak, journal, and think your reality into existence with your words on your side! Consciously changing your internal and external dialogue will extend to your unconscious world, the world around you, and effectively re-shape the linguistic content of your mind. Speak about what you want rather than what you don't. Focus on what is going right rather than what is going wrong. When you think to yourself, "I don't have any money," the unconscious generates the concept of you having no money. It doesn't understand that when you think that, you are actually thinking "I want more money." Why double your work? En-lighten-ment is just that – the raising of your vibration, and a lightening of your mental and emotional load via understanding.

The unconscious also makes associations and learns quickly. As your primary protector, the unconscious remains alert and on guard, gleaning survival lessons from every experience. Perhaps you associate school with stress. Perhaps you had a bad experience, and your subconscious subsequently made the association between schooling and stress. Perhaps the next time you encounter school you have an immediate physical reaction – one that you can't really consciously account for, but a very immediate and visceral reaction, nonetheless. "Neurons that fire together wire together," or so it goes, and in fact, yes they do.

Have you ever been a smoker? If you have, or if you are, you'll be able to recount all the ways in which your neurons have fired together and thus wired together. Driving in the car? Smoke. Having a beer? Smoke. Just finished a big dinner? Smoke. Obviously, addiction is a factor, but the triggers are those things that are subject to the "fire together wire together" notion. Hardwiring won't be undone in a day or two - you must painstakingly repeat the process until you achieve your desired result. Oftentimes you must first "unlearn" your current wiring, simply by being aware of it as it happens, resisting the urge to respond to the prompt, and then rewiring your neurons in the fashion of your choosing. For this reason, teachers and coaches are very specific about proper technique and form when you first begin a sport or an instrument (or whatever another undertaking).

In the beginning, your attention must be to the finer details, so as to effectively write them into your muscle memory. Once you've done that, you can relax and move on to the next task, because your body will do the rest. If, however, you code improper technique into your muscle memory, the process of correcting it is far more arduous.

If your coach or your teacher tells you PLAY SLOW, it's for your own efficiency later on. The secret beneath any practice in which you must repeat until the point of mastery is to believe in the process of repetition. Many people give up before they begin to see results because they don't believe in what they cannot see. If you plant a seed, do you see it germinate? No, but yet you trust and expect that it will eventually sprout, assuming that you take proper care to nurture it. Believing in the process and acting on that belief is the most effective way to yield the desired result.

VISUALIZATION

Intentional visualization is often overlooked, if not disregarded entirely as an efficient personal practice for everyday life. Neuroscience tells us that when you imagine yourself doing something, your brain reacts in the same way to that visualization as if you were you to perform the action in real life. Obviously, then, visualization has an effect on the mind, the brain and subsequently, the body.

"As we shall see, the most remarkable feature of imagery work is that it can be accompanied by physiological changes. The beneficial physical effects of imagery would not be so surprising if we commonly thought of those mental and physical aspects as comprising two sides of a mirror that we term "body." But for three hundred years, Western medicine has separated the mind from the body. You may be surprised to learn that no other medical system in the history of the world, including Western medicine prior to the seventeenth century, makes such a distinction." - Gerald Epstein, "Healing Visualizations: Creating Health through Imagery."

There are a plethora of stories of people who have achieved the miraculous via belief and visualization. Miraculous healings, extraordinary situations and shocking achievements reached with the power of the mind have been documented around the world and throughout human history. Here is one such story on the power of belief, or the "placebo effect":

"I was particularly inspired by a recorded lecture given by Caroline Myss. She told the story of a little boy with an inoperable, malignant brain tumor. He was given only months to live, but fortunately, his oncologist suggested to his parents that he try visualizing – the only hope the physician could offer. At his parents' urging, the little boy quickly adopted a daily visualization practice. He was about eight years old and was very much interested in Star Wars. Every morning this little boy would get up and go into a meditation, during which he visualized himself as a starship captain. Every day, he would shoot at the other starships. One morning as he was visualizing, he blew up his enemy's biggest star ship. He said nothing about this to his parents. The next morning, the young lad's mother came into his bedroom and asked him to do his visualizations. He told his mother that there was no need to do them anymore. He calmly informed her that his tumor was gone. It had been blown up! Not believing him, the boy's mother pressed him to meditate, which he dutifully did. Two weeks later, the boy went to his oncologist and was given a clean bill of health. The tumor was gone. He was completely cancer free." – Lissa Rankin, M.D. "Mind Over Medicine"

Regarding the concept of visualization and manifestation, the emotions are like the wind in the sails of your vessel. Visualize a situation that you desire, and really put yourself there -

experience it in your mind as viscerally as possible. Now, add emotion. Think about the energy that is contained within the realm of emotion – when you are ecstatic, what is your corresponding body state? How much momentum is contained within the purest joy or the deepest love? How much momentum lies within rage? Shame? Fear? If you find yourself in a situation where you are ruminating and overwhelmed by negative emotions, and you really want out, do your best to change course as quickly as possible to the next best option. Sometimes the mind is too tired to effectively lift itself from the undertow, but the body is there to help! The body is to mind as space is to time – the connection is inherent and holistic. The dualism of Descartes is a thing of the past, and in service of healthier communities, we must consider the elements of the human being holistically, and navigate accordingly for the future. If your mind needs help, enlist your body!

Change your activity, go for a walk, listen to music, watch a movie – get out of your mind, and if the body needs help, enlist the mind!

We know, without needing to be told, that our emotions have physiological effects. When you are angry, you FEEL it in your body. When you are sad you also feel it in your body, and the same goes for every other emotion. On some level or another, your emotional state affects your physical state, which affects your mental state, which affects your physiological state, which affects your emotional state, and so on.

DID YOU KNOW?

Over the span of the past fifty years, and more specifically, the past fifteen years, scientists have verified that the source of pain and anxiety symptoms are most often a result of what is now referred to as "cellular memory." Cellular memory is really just what we call memory, but researchers began adding the word "cellular," because although science had previously held that all memories are stored in the brain, surgeons began to find that even when they had, cumulatively and among many patients, removed every part of the brain, memory still remained. The experiences of organ transplant recipients also supports this idea:

"One famous example is Claire Sylvia, who wrote about her experience in the book "A Change of Heart." After her heart and lung transplant at Yale-New Haven Hospital in 1988, she noticed significant personality changes: she experienced strong cravings for Kentucky Fried Chicken, which as a health-conscious dancer and choreographer she would have never eaten before; she suddenly liked blues and greens rather than the bright reds and oranges she typically wore; and she became aggressive in her behavior, which was even more out of character. After some investigation, she discovered that all these new personality traits were characteristic of her donor. Dozens of similar experiences by other organ transplant recipients have been reported as well. The explanation is cellular memory." – Dr. Alexander Lloyd

In 2004, the "Dallas Morning News" ran a story called "Medical School Breakthrough," about a new study conducted at Southwestern University Medical Center in Dallas. Scientists had discovered that our experiences are recorded at the cellular level throughout our bodies, and they believed that these memories were the true source of illness and disease.

"Scientists believe these cellular memories might mean the dif-ference between a healthy life and death... Cancer can be the result of a bad cellular memory replacing a good one... This may provide

one of the most powerful ways of curing illness."
– Eric Nestler, MD

As we progress through the 21st century, science and medicine are making huge leaps in understanding illness, wellness, the mind, and the body. Scientists are finding, all over the natural world, cells and organisms that record their experiences without the benefit of a brain.

Research scientist Bruce Lipton discovered, while cloning human cells, that individual muscle cells react and change based on their "perception" of an environment, and not necessarily the actual environment. (What is an "actual" environment anyway, right? Dogs can't see rainbows, color-blind people can't perceive colors that others can, etc....). Lipton's research led to the idea that human beings, as a whole, react and change based on our perceptions of, or beliefs about, our environments, and he believes that virtually every health problem originates from an errant belief on the unconscious level.

"A cellular memory that triggers fear always goes back to a wrong interpretation of the original event. The true source of my fear and stress is not the fact that Mom died; it's my belief that because Mom died, I'll never be okay again. It's not the diagnosis of cancer; it's my belief that because I've been diagnosed with cancer, my life is over. It's not the unkind thing someone did to me in and of itself; it's my belief that this unkind thing means that I am a person of inferior worth and value." – Dr. Alexander Lloyd

Dr. Lloyd goes on to reference the book, "Is This Your Child?" in which Doris Rapp writes on a cellular memory idea called the "barrel effect." Consider all of life's stress as being one big internal barrel. As long as the barrel is not full, our body can deal with new stress. Once our barrel is full, however, the littlest thing could cause a meltdown.

"Our stress barrel also includes generational memories. One could have had an idyllic childhood and a trauma-free life, but for some reason still have significant confidence issues, depression issues, health issues, or addictions. I've worked with many people who fit into that category, who later learn that a significant trauma occurred generations back—for example, a child was hit by a train and died—and no one in the family was ever the same again. These cellular memories, which are pow-erful human hard-drive viruses, are passed down like DNA. The more adrenaline released when the event happens, the stronger the cellular memory is, the more it affects you, and the more likely it is to be passed onto fu-ture generations. So the memories affecting you may not even be yours. Generational memories can explain the existence of what we started -calling "the cycle" and "breaking the cycle" a few decades back, or the behavior thought, and feeling patterns that keep repeating in certain families." – Lloyd

Karen Lawson, M.D., suggests that when we express our emotions without any attachment or judgment, we give them the freedom to flow out of our bodies and release the weight of this heavier energy. Holding onto toxic thoughts can cause a variety of problems such as high blood pressure and digestive troubles. Chronic stress can actually decrease your lifespan by shortening your telomeres (the "end caps" of DNA strands, which have a big impact on aging).

Every time you have a negative thought, your brain creates more synapses and pathways in alignment with your thought process at the time – so thinking predominantly negative thoughts will only breed more of them, while the adverse is true as well. According to many scientists, negative thinking and emotions inhibit signals from being transmitted between the central nervous system and the brain.

IMPROVE YOUR MINDSET

The sum total of all the people in the world today can be broken down into two groups, those who are always able to find success at everything they do, and those that, despite any skills or talents they may have, can never seem to get going properly. This is so because the first group has a mindset that encourages personal growth while the other does not.

The truth of the matter is that there are two very different ways people are raised when it comes to understanding ability and intelligence. Those who always seem to lack the motivation for success believe that talent and intelligence are innate and what you are born with is all you will ever get while the other, more successful, group believes that they are simply skills and that like any other skill then can be obtained via hard work and perseverance.

These two very different viewpoints, in turn, lead to dramatically different outlooks on life which eventually lead to extremely varying results. While this might seem hard to believe, for some of you anyway, heading out into the world each day with the understanding that success is possible as long as you put in the time and effort to find it will, in fact, lead to more success over time.

Known as the growth mindset, this is one thing that you can be sure all successful people have, and most of them had it instilled upon them at a very early age. At some point during childhood, everyone is either told that they succeed because they were naturally good at things or because they worked hard and never gave up.

Those who are told that they were naturally gifted often developed what is known as a fixed mindset which leads to their brains being the most active when they were receiving praise for how gifted they were. On the other hand, those that were told that their hard work was the key to their success developed what is known as a growth mindset which means their brains are most active when they are learning how to better themselves.

Fixed Mindset

- Wants to look smart or competent regardless of the reality
- Quick to avoid challenges
- Easily thwarted by obstacles
- Thinks effort is "pointless"

- Ignores feedback
- Can feel threatened by the success of others

Growth Mindset

- More interested in long-term results.
- Enjoys a challenge.
- Learns from obstacles
- Equates effort with success
- Appreciates criticism
- Finds inspiration in the success of others

To understand how the two mindsets work in action, simply remember the story of the tortoise and the hare. The hare was always told how fast he was and therefore developed a fixed mindset whereby his speed was innate and not related to his actions which meant he was free to take a nap during the race. The tortoise, on the other hand, kept a growth mindset which meant he knew that if he persevered he would succeed. This belief in himself was born out by the results of the race.

The two mindsets also manifest themselves differently when it comes to dealing with setbacks. When those who have a fixed mindset are met with a setback it directly affects how they see themselves because it shakes their belief in their innate talent. This makes it easier for them to give up on something they are struggling with as they can easily tell themselves that it is just not a talent that is in their wheelhouse. On the other hand, when a person with a growth mindset is met with a challenge they instead worry about the best way to overcome it and treat the issue as an opportunity to learn and grow.

MAXIMIZE YOUR NEUROPLASTICITY

With the consequences of having a fixed mindset so potentially disastrous, especially if you are striving to find the inner strength to empower yourself to improve your lot in life, it is important to do what you can to break these negative mental habits as quickly as possible. Luckily the human brain has the ability to constantly reshape itself throughout the course of its lifetime which means that it is never too late to shift into a growth mindset, no matter how deeply rooted the fixed mindset principles might be. New neural pathways in the brain can be formed as new thoughts are repeated time and again, and once they become well-worn paths, then new habits are formed.

While this same fact means that it will be much more difficult to change the habits that are already deeply ingrained, such as those that involve mentally keeping yourself from reaching an empowered state. While changing from a fixed to a growth mindset will be difficult, the tips outlined below will make the process more manageable than it might otherwise be.

Commit yourself to the task in front of you: Your mindset is one of the most deeply rooted patterns that your brain has gotten used to following through on over the years which means that if you ever want to empower yourself and improve it then you are really going to need to dedicate yourself to the process. It is important to keep in mind that this will be a marathon, not a sprint, and to set your expectations accordingly.

Begin with something simple: When it comes to creating new neural pathways, one of the best ways to do so is by seeing a noticeable result from an action that you consciously took in an effort to change your mindset. While a single positive choice or two a day won't generate noticeable results on their own, their cumulative effect can be substantial and that typing point can occur sooner than you might think.

Stay positive: When working to keep a growth mindset in all things, it is important to keep it up even when the going gets tough. It will likely seem like the easiest thing in the world to do while things are going well, but a fixed mindset is much more likely to manifest itself during times when roadblocks begin presenting themselves. Your fixed mindset will likely make you want to abandon all hope of forward progress when these road blocks appear.

In this case, it is important to make an effort to stop thinking of the challenges as roadblocks and start thinking of them as opportunities for you to learn and grow. Finding personal ways to meet the challenges that come your way head on without dwelling on them unnecessarily is the first step towards making a real change for the better. If you are having difficulty putting this idea into practice, consider the following:

Take the time to look for the silver lining and consider what opportunities that meeting this challenge head on will give you access to. Dealing with problems as soon as they arise will typically provide you with the opportunity to handle the issue in a simpler fashion or take actions to stop the situation from otherwise getting out of hand. Learning to appreciate this opportunity will make adopting a growth mindset much easier.

Use the challenge in question as a mirror to reflect challenges you might be having when looking to improve other facets of your life. If everything is going smoothly then it can be easy to overlook important information that could come back to bite you later if left untreated for too long. Dealing with challenges directly can, in turn, then provide you insight into what else in your life deserves a closer examination.

Think about why you feel the way you do. When

face to face with roadblocks, you will find that it is often easier to approach them with a growth mindset when you take an extra moment to stop and really consider them. A rundown of the facts will often reveal that the roadblock will be much easier to overcome than it first appeared, likely because of a personal bias that made it seem much more intimidating.

Avoiding negative self-talk: Self-criticism can be beneficial if restricted to a healthy measure. However, there is a limit to the amount of negative conditioning you can subject your mind to before it starts becoming counter-productive. There is a sea of difference between, "I really need to be more physically active" than "I am a lazy blob."

Excessive self-loathing can heavily backfire because it shifts the focus from ways through which we can improve to our failures. Over a longer period, thrash negative self-speak can up your stress level, and lead to major depression. Learning to tame negative self talk is the key to overcoming challenges, feeling more confident and achieving the life of your dreams. Keep in mind that "the only thing limiting us is our belief that there are limits." Here are some tried and tested techniques for tackling the negative self-talk monster.

Throw Negative Self-Talk Into A Box: Visualize your mistakes in a tiny box the next time you find yourself exaggerating each of them. For instance, if you find yourself underperforming at a meeting or presentation, rather than thinking, it's the end of your career, try rationalizing by criticizing your choice of words. "I could have used better words or my choice of words wasn't up to the mark." This really sounds more believable than "I screwed up my career." Visualize a small box and put your poor choice of words into it. You will subconsciously diminish the problem's size, and end up feeling way more confident.

Practice Possibility Thinking: If you are constantly thinking in extremely glowing terms, you may trigger the mental lie detector which tells you that you are functioning in a surreal world. Do not force yourself to resort to extremely unreal positive thoughts. Instead, take a neutral approach when you are besieged with negative thoughts. Be more neutral in your thinking. Think about the possibilities why a certain thing could have occurred. When you feel heavy and low on energy, instead of saying, "I am a fleshy seal or fat cow" or even, "I am a goddess or diva, irrespective of how I look" try saying, "I'd be really nice if I can knock off a few pounds. It will make me feel healthier, more energetic and fitter."

In order to transition between a fixed mindset and a growth mindset, the first thing you will want to do is to consider your daily life under a microscope in the hopes of picking up on destructive habits that may be limiting your mindset without your knowledge. Once you have found these negative habits, it will be easier to act against them directly.

Look back on every day: While you are first starting out, you will likely find that you have difficultly retaining a burgeoning growth mindset as the day wears on. If this is the case, you will likely find it helpful to keep a ledger tallying all of your growth and fixed mindset thoughts throughout the day. Simply keep track of each and pay special attention to the period of time that typifies a transition from positive to negative. While this may simply be a case of the day wearing on you, it may also be related to a specific event which you are not even aware of.

The only way you will know is if you map it all out in front of yourself every day for at least a month to provide you will all the data that you need to make an informed decision.

Have realistic expectations: Finally, you are going to want to keep in mind the fact that just because someone has a growth mindset doesn't mean that they are going to be happy about everything negative that befalls them. After all, everyone is simply going to have a bad day now and then; the important thing to remember is that while everyone might have an urge to give up when the going gets tough, those who have a growth mindset manage to ignore this feeling and preserve until they find the success that they have been searching for. It is important to compartmentalize these feelings rather than letting them dangerously spiral to the point that they are much more difficult to ignore than they might otherwise be. Don't let a moment of doubt turn into a day, an hour or even a minute, commit to change and find the growth mindset hiding inside you right now.

TRY AFFIRMATIONS

One great way to cut these negative thoughts off at the root is with the power of repetition. Repetition is useful when it comes to bypassing the mental filters that your fixed mindset has been allowed to create over the years when it comes to deciding how you are going to act, by default, in a given situation. Repetition is especially effective because it can allow new thoughts to slip past these filters, putting you on the path to neuroplasticity in the process.

Affirmations or mantras, positive sentences which are repeated throughout the day, are a great place to start. Affirmations are written down while mantras are repeated either aloud or in your head and both make it easier to block out any negative static that your fixed mindset has to contribute in a given situation.

When you are first stating out with this practice, it is natural to feel foolish, or as though you are wasting your time. While these thoughts are perfectly natural, if you make the mistake of acting on them, then you will be allowing your fixed mindset to assert its dominance and prevent you from making positive changes in your own life. When you are feeling especially dispirited and as though you arcn't making any forward progress, it is important to power through these feelings as they are just your fixed mindset fight back. The longer you don't interact with these thoughts, the less likely they are to return.

To ensure you don't bite off more than you can chew all at once, it is recommended that you start off with an affirmation or mantra that is fairly close to your current mental comfort zone. Starting with something small will make it easier to rewire your brain in a positive direction when compared to starting with something serious right off the bat.

I Am Me: Affirmations of Self-Love

- I am a loving person who deserves to be loved in return.

- I demand respect from people around me and give respect in return.

- I am kind and caring, and I deserve to be happy.

- I am deserving of respect and admiration from my peers.

- I deserve love and kindness from those around me.

- I love the person I am just the way that I am.

- I strive to be a better person every day.

- I am worthy of love, kindness, and respect from my peers.

- I feel good about myself as an individual.

- I feel good about myself as a friend, companion, and family member.

- I am good enough for those around me.

- I am accepting and accepted by my peers.

- I am the perfect me, regardless of others'

expectations.

- I set my own expectations for myself, meeting and exceeding them.

- I expect my best in any given situation, and I give my best.

I Am Assertive: Affirmations of Self-Confidence

- I am responsible and accountable for only my own actions and reactions.

- I show my gratitude and thankfulness in new and positive ways.

- I am grateful for the positive people and energy in my life.

- I only allow positivity to affect my mental

well-being.

- I only allow honesty and loyalty from those around me.

I Am Fearless: Affirmations of Courage

- I am capable of pursuing and achieving my goals.

- I always put forth my best efforts in all aspects of my life.

- I am not deterred from my short and long-term goals.

- I accept changes in my life without fear of failure or rejection.

- I emit positive energies and attract positive energies in return.

- I am brave in the face of adversity.

- I face challenges head-on and without fear.

I Am Driven: Affirmations of Ambition

- My strong work ethic is an asset to my career goals.

- I am an asset to my job and worthy of advancement to higher levels of responsibility.

- I accept constructive criticism with an open mind and heart.

- I am strong and determined to forge my own paths in life.

- I reject negative criticism in a positive

manner without taking it to heart.

- I approach problem-solving with a firm belief in my abilities.

- I work hard and deserve recognition for that hard work.
- I demand no less than what my skill set is worth.

- I strive to improve my skill set every day.

- I reject negativity in the workplace, and I embrace positivity.

I Am Personable: Affirmations of Social Engagement

- I am charming and people enjoy being around me.

- I do not allow my anxiety to build a wall around me.

- I am funny and love to make people laugh.

- I do not shy away from new surroundings and new people.

- I enjoy meeting new people with like-minded spirits.

I Am Enough: Affirmations of Self-Acceptance

- I embrace the differences in my body that make me unique.

- My quirky sense of humor brings light and laughter to my life and the lives of my peers.

- I am beautiful on the inside and the outside.

- I am fortunate to be mentally and physically healthy.

- I am cautious and approach situations with an observant and open mind.

Chapter 3: The Most Complicated Object In The Known Universe

"The human brain has 100 billion neurons, each neuron connected to ten thousand other neurons. Sitting on your shoulders is the most complicated object in the known universe." – Michio Kaku

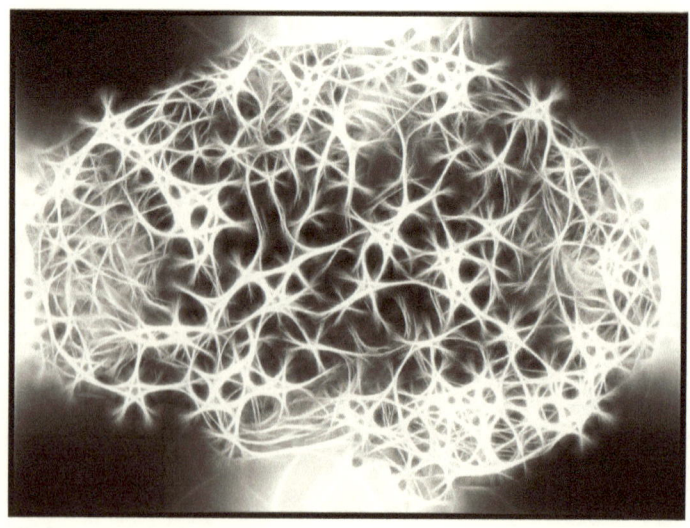

It is the brain's ability to change itself that makes it so incredible, and it should follow that if you are your body, and your body is you, then you are your brain and your brain is you. Therefore, your ability to change yourself is what makes you incredible. Great power is the ceaseless ability to adapt to circumstances and to change, and the evolutionary notion of "survival of the fittest" is just that; the fittest are those capable of the evolution necessary to move forward. Evolution waits for no one.

Until the late twentieth century, the brain was thought to have been similar to a machine – something fixed and compartmentalized by the age of eighteen, but we now know that the brain is intrinsically plastic, which means that it is literally never not plastic; whether you are one or one hundred, your brain can, does and will change itself in the moment, as you think, and as you interact with your environment.

Neuroplasticity, essentially, is the brain's ability to reorganize itself by forming new neural connections over time via repetition.

If you want to rewire your brain, repetition is paramount.

Your brain is incredible.

It's amazing.

If we were to build a computer that could simulate a human brain, it would be the size of a city block, it would require a nuclear power plant to energize it, and a lake to cool it, and yet our brains are housed in our comparatively tiny heads, and powered solely by our bodies.

Regardless of how you feel about yourself or your life, you are housing one of the most powerful and mysterious things in the universe, and not only that, you are the one powering it. You ARE your brain and your brain IS you, so you should be very proud!

THE PLASTIC BRAIN

Paul Bach-y-Rita is known as the leading visionary of neuroplasticity, and the first to propose the concept of "sensory substitution" to treat patients with neurological issues. The notion of sensory substitution is, essentially, that you feed the brain sensory information via one sense, and the hypothesis is that the brain will use and redirect that information appropriately, and, given time and repetition, more efficiently. Imagine that the information traveling around the brain is taking the "major routes," or "highways," but if an accident occurs somewhere and one of the highways becomes inoperable, the brain must re-route the information via "back roads." It must recruit, rewire, re-design, and re-plan. The more that the information travels these "back roads," the sooner these roads become the new highways.

One of the first applications of sensory substitution created by Bach-y-Rita was a chair that allowed blind people to 'see.' The trials he conducted in 1969 are now considered to be the first form of experimental evidence for neuroplasticity, and an illustration of the feasibility of sensory substitution.

Bach-y-Rita's chair had a bank of four hundred vibrating plates resting against the user's back and vibrating in connection with a camera placed above the chair facing forwards. The pattern in which the stimulation occurred enabled the user to "see," often being able to recognize an object coming toward the camera (illustrate with photos). Bach-y-Rita expected that this was neuroplasticity in action, and eventually, as technologies improved, scientists were able to prove, via brain scan, that the brain truly is plastic.

Bach-y-Rita also created a device which enabled patients with damaged vestibular nuclei (constant wobbling and the inability to remain upright) to regain their ability to remain balanced by using an electrical stimulator placed on the tongue, which reacted to a motion sensor affixed to the patient. This application enabled patients to remain balanced without the equipment after several weeks of use, indicating the strengthening of the new neural "highways" via time and repetition.

The device used by Bach-y-Rita, now sold as "Brainport," consists of a group of accelerometers attached to the patient and linked to a computer. The information is then processed and fed to a small plate positioned on the patient's tongue (due to the density of sensory receptors on the tongue). The device stimulates different areas of the tongue depending on the orientation of the accelerometers, the information is sent to the "touch" center of the brain, and is then re-routed by the brain accordingly. This stimulation allows the patient to stay balanced, and after repeated use, Bach-y-Rita discovered that the patient remained balanced for a short time after using the device.

After using the device for several weeks, the patient was completely cured, illustrating yet another application of neuroplasticity in treating neurological disorders, and also the ability of the brain to adapt to repeated stimuli. The duration was also a factor, in that the longer the patient did the exercise, the longer she was able to remain balanced after the treatment until she was fully able to return to her regular life.

This was only the seventies, at the dawn of the discovery of neuroplasticity.

It gets even crazier.

Lieutenant James Holman was a man who had become blind in his twenties as a result of chronic health troubles that began during his time in the navy. More notable, however, are the journeys and tales of his life AFTER he had become blind. James Holman, while blind, spent the majority of his life traveling the world.... alone. He trekked, by foot, across the majority of Siberia. He also mapped the Australian Outback, crossed the Indian Ocean via cargo ship, and climbed Mount Vesuvius mid-eruption, and those are only a few of his adventures. In total, he travelled 250,000 miles, which would be the equivalent of ten trips around the Equator.

He did all of this completely blind and alone.

How did he accomplish such a feat?

Holman had a few tricks to help him out – using coins as currency rather than bills, a special pocket watch that allowed him to tell time, a dictation machine to document his travels, and most magnificently, Holman had taught himself echolocation using a hickory cane, and he had re-wired his brain. It took years of determined work, and obviously, it took unwavering belief, intent, action, and repetition.

How did it work?

Imagine the sound of the cane clacking on the concrete and reaching Holman's ear. First of all, the sound vibrates the bones and membranes within his ear canal, and then the sound wave transfers its energy to a fluid in his inner ear. The fluid then sloshes over the rows of little hair cells, and bends some of them to a greater or lesser extent, depending on the sound. The hairs are connected to the dendrites of nearby nerve cells, which then fire, and transmit electrical signals through the axons and to the brain. Upon reaching the brain, the signal causes the axon to release chemicals into a nearby synapse. This arouses neurons in the auditory cortex, a patch of grey matter in the temporal lobe, where the sound is "heard."

For Holman, however, the experience doesn't end there. In order for him to consciously navigate with the sound, the signal must circulate through other patches of grey matter for further processing. Reaching that grey matter, however, requires a dive beneath the grey matter surface, and into the white matter of the brain.

Information moving within the white matter moves at speeds of up to 250 miles per hour, because the axons that move the information from one gray matter node to another are fatter than other axons, and axons are also sheathed in a fatty substance called "myelin" which insulates the axon, making the transfer of information that much more efficient. Consider the grey matter as a patchwork of chips that analyze different types of information and the white matter as cables that transmit information between those chips.

So basically, Holman's brain had to re-route the signal through the white matter to different patches of grey matter, but how do the signals know which path to take? In the same way as walking a trail through the bushes, again and again, will eventually carve out a path, so do signals in the brain follow these paths within its landscape. Really, all Holman had to do was "try" to learn echolocation, and continue to practice, and his brain did the rest of the work.

When one neuron causes another to fire over and over, the synapse between them changes in response. The axon tip of one neuron expands and begins acquiring more neurotransmitters to flood the synapse between the neurons. New axon branches may also sprout. The neuron that has been influenced, then, may lend attention back to the influencing neuron by extending more dendrite receptors toward it. Over time, the influenced neuron will respond to even mild prompts, as a pathway is forged.

Whenever Holman would click his cane, the sound waves that bounced off of various objects reached his ear at varying times. With literally years and years of repetition and practice, Holman was able to image the world around him in his mind as his brain learned to triangulate the time differences and determine the layout of the scenery surrounding him. Eventually, he could evaluate details about an object's size, shape, and texture, essentially mastering the sensory capacity of echolocation.

The brain is a remarkable thing, and even with brain scans and technology, and all of our advanced information, there remain cases of incredible feats and stories that defy logic. One such story, as referenced in Oliver Sacks' "Musicophilia," is the case of Tony Cicoria, a forty-two year old orthopedic surgeon living in a small city in upstate New York.

One afternoon Tony was attending a family gathering at a lakeside pavilion when a storm began to move in.

He went to use a pay phone outside the pavilion to make a quick call to his mother, and when he'd hung up the phone, a flash of light erupted from the phone and struck him in the face.

He'd been struck by lightning.

"I was flying forwards. Bewildered. I looked around. I saw my own body on the ground. I said to myself, 'oh shit, I'm dead.' I saw people converging on the body. I saw a woman – she had been standing waiting to use the phone right behind me – position herself over my body, give it CPR...I floated up to the stairs – my consciousness came with me. I saw my kids, had the realization that they would be okay. Then I was surrounded by a bluish-white light... an enormous feeling of well-being and peace. No emotion associated with these...pure thought, pure ecstasy. I had the perception of accelerating, being drawn up...there was speed and direction. Then, as I was saying to myself, 'this is the most glorious feeling I've ever had' – SLAM! I was back."

Upon waking, and after having had neurological

and medical examinations, it seemed that nothing was really awry with, as perplexing as that was. He'd experienced a few memory issues here and there, but otherwise, he was back to his regular life.

However...

He began experiencing an insatiable desire to listen to piano music, which was out of the ordinary for him as he hadn't really had much interest prior to his accident. He'd had a few piano lessons as a kid, but nothing notable and no interest in his adult life. He began buying recordings of the piano music of Chopin and subsequently ended up ordering all of the sheet music.

"Coincidentally" enough, one of his babysitters at the time asked him if she could store her old piano at his house, and he began to teach himself to play.

He then began to hear music in his head,

"The first time, it was a dream. I was in a tux, onstage; I was playing something I had written. I woke up, startled, and the music was still in my head." So he jumped out of bed and started trying to write it down, hardly knowing how to even notate it, and whenever he would sit down to attempt some Chopin, his own music would "come and take me over. It had a very powerful presence."

He eventually became possessed by it, obsessed; it was like the music insisted it be released. He'd wake up at four am and play until he had to go to work, and get back to it at the end of the day – it was endless. The music took over his life, and it came in "an absolute torrent of notes with no breaks, no rests between them, and he would have to give it shape and form." – Sacks

MUSIC AND THE BRAIN

"Musical activity involves nearly every region of the brain that we know of and nearly every neural subsystem." – Daniel Levitin, "This is Your Brain on Music"

How do we even begin to discuss the relationship between music and the brain? It's a romance. When music and the brain get together they're all over each other – they become one; they entrain. Music is one of the most immediate and powerful ways in which you can change your brain, your mind, your body, and your spirit because it floods your entire being in an instant. Your heart entrains to the rhythm, your body can't help but move, your breathing entrains, and may even follow the vocals (depending on whether you are hearing or listening), engaging your body as you engage in the experience. Your entire brain lights up to the stem, influencing the rest of your being. The deeper you engage, the deeper and more profound your results. We are energy, everything is energy, and music is energy intended. We all know how it feels to purge an emotion through a song or to celebrate within one. How cathartic is it to listen to music and to let it envelop you; to surrender. Is it your perception of "you," that likes music, or is it the "you" of your brain? Your body? Your mind? Your bodymind? Either way, the surrender of the human being to music, and the relationship between music and the brain is unique, and the shift in consciousness, depending on the music, is immediate, due to the entrainment of the brain and body. Music gives neuroplasticity wings, and a simple, everyday example of this is the alphabet song. Learning something by memory, dry, will take far longer than putting that same activity to a song.

Visualization of music is extremely powerful. Dare we dip into the secrets?! Let's begin with a basic example from an experiment done by neuroscientists on the power of imagery itself. The scientists had people sit at a piano and play a five-finger scale repeatedly, and they mapped the brains of the subjects while they played. The parts of the brain involved in the activity grew the more that the subjects practiced. The scientists then had another group sit at the piano and simply visualize the same experience.

The brain scans were identical.

When you listen to music, try listening to it in headphones, and actually listening to it actively, in that you put yourself at the helm of the experience. As you listen, visualize yourself AS the vocalist, or as the drummer, or the guitarist, or whatever it is – play along in your mind as the song plays into your head. Follow it with your emotion, really "be" there in it and experience it as viscerally as possible. Note your physiology afterwards.

Try it.

Not only does it feel amazing, but it activates your entire brain, body and mind, your emotions... everything, which is most likely why it feels amazing. If we had to reduce this entire book to one word, as an answer to "how to change your mind," that word would be music.

The subject of the relationship between music and the brain is vast, and far too extensive to touch on in this book, but let's briefly touch on some of the direct physiological effects of your own voice on yourself.

Chapter 4: The Body - The Unconscious Mind?

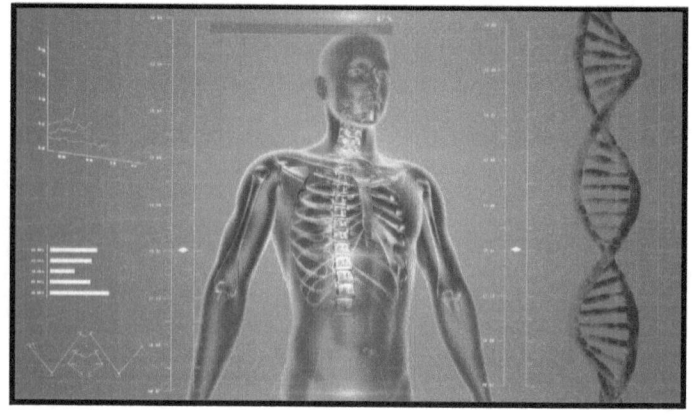

What is the collective unconscious but the "knowledge" that we've held as collectives over time? Consider the concept of Dualism, which is essentially the notion that the body and mind are separate entities. Dualism is still an infant in terms of the span of time in which humanity has existed, yet in our culture, it has remained long enough for us to forget about it and to have banked it into our collective unconscious as a "truth." Consider the body itself as the unconscious mind – makes sense, no? What are the things that you do unconsciously? It's all body function, right? Because anything conscious we call "mind" – everything else we call "body," but really, that's only because that belief is now a part of the "muscle memory" of our collective unconscious. You know those "random" thoughts that you might have, maybe you are at the grocery store and you have an overwhelming desire to buy black beans despite the fact that you rarely eat them (but maybe that's why...?), or you get a random thought to buy pickles.. but maybe not so random if you aren't one to remember to tend to your gut microbiota. Or perhaps you have a recurring body issue, and suddenly have this "strange" thought to forgive that body part. Just because the conscious mind doesn't think it doesn't mean that 'you' don't' think it – that random thought to buy pickles, or to forgive your body, or the longing for black beans... that was "you." You ARE your body. Your body knows how to get what it wants in as much as you know how to get what you want because your body is you. Our bodies are intelligent, they think, they store knowledge, hold memory, process information, change, and adapt as we interact with our environments. You are your body and your body is you. Here's an interesting exercise to try:

The next time that you speak about your body (the unconscious) "doing" something, change the focus from the "body" doing it, to "you" doing it. "You" digested your dinner, "you" washed yourself while you slept (brain), "you" activated your fight-or-flight response when you reached into your pocket for your keys and they weren't there, "you" pumped blood through your arteries this morning, and in fact, you are never not pumping blood through your arteries because it seems that you're obsessed with doing it. It's just something that you clearly enjoy; it's one of your most favorite activities, one would assume, as you literally do it twenty-four seven. What else are you obsessed with? You LOVE to use oxygen – all day long you do it, dutifully turning oxygen into carbon dioxide and churning it out. Others may wonder what's up with all the oxygen churning if they weren't also obsessed with it and doing it all day every day themselves.

Your relationship with your unconscious is your own, but there are many ways to get in touch with your body. Even the simple exercise of considering your bodily functions to be functions that you yourself are purposefully doing is enough to further ignite the dialogue between you and your body, or to be more concise, the dialogue between you and yourself. The disconnect is that these processes are unconscious and we are therefore unaware of them, but to consider those processes as "your" own and not "your body's" processes, is almost novel, as much as it seems to be common sense.

The notion that the mind and body are separate is an illustration of the repetition, over time, of the pervading concept of Dualism.

BREATHING

So what are some ways in which we can begin to master the unconscious that is our bodies? Let's begin with breathing.

If you survey a group of athletes and ask them about their experience of intentional breathing and how it relates to their performance and practice, the answers are overwhelmingly unanimous in that their relationship with their breath is a fundamental part, if not at the core of their practice. For those who participate in sports or in activities where the body is the focus, breathing is a fundamental element, and the greater the mastery of the breath and of its breadth, depth and potential, the greater the physical feats, stamina, endurance and mastery. It is your breath, after all that animates you, sustains you, and makes you what you are. You can last weeks without food, days without water, but breath exists in the realm of minutes and hours.

"Breathe," is perhaps another one-word answer to the question of how to change your mind.

Let's examine the physiology of breathing and the effects of intentional breathing on the bodymind. Intentional breathing contributes to relaxation, stress management, improvement of organ function, and overall control of psycho-physiological states.

The "pre-Botzinger" complex or "preBotC" is the name of a cluster of neurons in the brainstem discovered in nineteen ninety-one by a neurology professor at UCLA. The cluster was first discovered in mice but has since been applied to the human brain as well. In 2016, scientists Mark Krasnow and Kevin Yackle identified and studied the preBotC neurons that affected sighing in mice. Their latest findings are focusing on how these neurons affect breathing, emotional states, and alertness or arousal. The scientists have discovered the exciting correlation between breathing and changes in emotional state, not that we weren't already aware of that (taking deep breaths to calm down, for example), but it can now be observed and measured, as scientists have now located the neural circuit that causes us to calm when we breathe slowly and deeply.

Breath work, yoga, and meditation are ways in

which to combat the effect of modern stress on our bodies, as the physiological effects experienced during meditation counteract those experienced during stress. This includes sports, martial arts, and many other endeavors where focused and intentional breathing is at the core of the practice. Breathing is like a connecting link between the "body" and "mind," or, rather, the "conscious" and the "unconscious."

Breathing is unique in that it is both an unconscious function and a controllable function. Can you manipulate your endocrine system at will? Perhaps one day... but for now, we have our breath – one of our most powerful allies. Breathing communicates with the entire body and is a fundamental part of our unconscious activity. You have access to it immediately! You can immediately slow or accelerate your breathing at will, thus affecting the rest of your body. Slower breathing slows the body down, allowing for changes in a brain wave state, emotional state, perceptual state, and physiological state, and accelerating breathing excites the systemic functions and increases oxygen flow throughout the body.

Varying brain wave states can be accessed via intentional breathing.

The Delta wave state, which vibrates at between zero point five and four hertz, is the slowest brain wave state, and it is the state of deep sleep in adults. Babies between the ages of zero and two exist in the delta wave state, and it is an ideal state for unconscious programming.

Theta waves vibrate at between four and eight hertz and are the typical brainwave state during meditation. The theta state is associated with visualization, heightened intuition, and occurs in the primary stage of sleep. Children between the ages of two and six operate in the theta wave state – the realm of the imagination. This is a state in which an individual is open to suggestion (hypnosis), and will readily accept what they are told is true.

Alpha waves vibrate between eight and thirteen hertz, and the Alpha state is a state of relaxation. Children between the ages of five and eight are in the Alpha wave state, and it is associated with creativity, inspiration, ideas, and learning. The Alpha state could be considered the "gap" between the conscious and the unconscious; the portal between.

Beta waves vibrate between fourteen and twenty-nine hertz, and the Beta wave state is the typically alert waking state – the realm of conscious, analytical thinking. Children enter the Beta state after the age of eight.

Gamma waves vibrate between thirty and one

hundred hertz and are the brain waves involved in higher processing tasks and cognitive functioning. Gamma waves contribute to active learning, memory, information processing, and hyperactivity and the gamma wave state is the ideal state in which to retain information. Stimulation coupled with learning, therefore, can be a potentially valuable practice.

Notice that brain wave states operate in cycles per second, as do sounds...
We will touch on meditation again in the final chapter of this book, but for now let's head back into the archives of the unbelievable with a story of belief, intention, action, and the will to sustain the process of achieving the incredible.

"When people hear my dream of swimming in the Olympics and I tell them I want to be like Michael Phelps, people laugh ... They say, 'You are a refugee and you get £5 a day, don't waste your time and do other things.' But I believe in myself and that I can do anything. When I hear people say that, it pushes me harder. I am not just a refugee, but I am a dreamer." – Eid Al Jazairi

Do you know how sometimes your greatest obstacles become your greatest allies? So was the case for Eid Al Jazairi, a twenty-five year old Syrian refugee who fled Damascus to Britain in 2016. At the time, Eid had to cross the Mediterranean in a tiny boat, and when he arrived in Britain three years ago he wasn't able to swim. Now, he swims competitively and hopes to compete in the 2020 Olympics in Tokyo.

Al Jazairli had been training to be an accountant, and working as a visual merchandiser when the Syrian war broke out, and he arrived in Britain on a five-year visa in 2016 where he moved into a hostel. It all began one night while hanging out at a friend's place in north-east London, and he happened to catch a YouTube video of American swimmer Michael Phelps. It lit him up immediately, and after watching two hours of film, he decided that swimming was something he had to do.

Within six months he was clocking forty-three seconds for the fifty-meter freestyle, and his coaches suspect he could compete on a refugee team if the Rio 2016 innovation is repeated at the 2020 games in Tokyo.

Al Jazairli lives on an allowance of five pounds per day, and he saves on groceries to put money aside for his monthly gym membership. When he began his practice, he couldn't swim more than two or three meters, but he swims daily between six and eight am and six and eight pm. He says that swimming takes him away from everything and brings him to a world where he is untouchable.

So what was the fundamental ingredient here? Was it swimming repetitions? Was it the fact that he had a coach? His trip across the Mediterranean? His upbringing? His genes? Or was the fundamental ingredient of the decision that he made within himself to dream his dream into life? A silent knowing that he boldly acted upon.

"I'm a dreamer." – Eid Al Jazairi

FOOD

Ok, food is another one of those "one-word answers." Food is huge – food is life, it is fuel, it is medicine. That much is undeniable, wherever on the spectrum your views fall. In the West, food USED to be considered medicine, wasn't it Hippocrates that said "let thy food be thy medicine," and don't western doctors take a "Hippocratic Oath?" What does that even mean anymore? Typically, hospital food in North America is the LAST priority as far as health. In fact, food is essentially overlooked as an option for healing and is merely tended to as an obligatory practice. Here, here's your obligatory T.V. dinner for the night. Here's your "fruit" cup. It's 2019, let's not pretend that packaged food is the same as food from the ground, not that there isn't a spectrum, but it's not absurd to say that the closer to the earth that the food is, the more valuable it will be for the body, and as it moves across the spectrum of source, it can go the opposite way as well. How many "foods" now are actually essentially poisons? We can pretend we don't know but come on, we are organic beings, there's no way that inorganic substances are sustenance. Your body is just so intelligent and capable, that it fights off what you give it, around the clock. If you are eating packaged foods and fast foods around the clock, you are essentially forcing your body to be on the battlefield, around the clock. Would you give your dog a Big Mac? Probably not, right? But can you give dogs fruits, vegetables and meant? Yep! Just because we "can" eat something doesn't mean that we should. The FDA approves things that won't kill you – that doesn't mean that these things will vitalize you, and not that we don't all participate in our own ways in the variety of foods and non-foods that are out there, but understanding what is and isn't food and how it is received by your body is a beneficial practice.

That being said, how easy is it to access REAL food when you live, let's say, in small town suburbia? Or in downtown, low-income neighborhoods with fast food places and convenience stores on every corner. How about the general imbalance in the food system at large? One that is tough for the individual to navigate, without appropriate resources. So many cycles of imbalance have been born of the industrial revolution, of colonialism, of capitalism, etc.... and we are waking up to find that what we've been sold as "food," isn't, and the harmful "food" is far more affordable, available, and marketed. Our societal system is a system of scarcity in the name of "profit." Why don't companies make things that last forever? Because there's no money in that; sustainability doesn't generate profit. It's not impossible, it just isn't profitable.

Well, guess what! There's nothing profitable about exhausting our resources until we are at the point where we are not even just contemplating, but PLANNING to terraform the asteroid belt.

How much of a testament to the modern western view of health is hospital food!

Just because someone in a white coat tells you some kind of "truth" about your body doesn't mean that it overrules YOUR truths about your body. Your truths are equally valid as you participate with your doctor in service of your health. People just regurgitate what they learn – having letters after your name doesn't make anyone an authority on the experience of anyone else – it just makes them informative on the subject matter, and, depending on their approach, a potentially helpful ally in your healing experience.

What if a study came out tomorrow from the most reputable source around, saying that the majority of what doctors have learned in medical school is archaic information and is in need of an overhaul. Would you believe it? Ask yourself how much "authority" someone else needs to appear to have in order to overthrow your own authority on yourself.

"In Western medicine, the body is seen as a machine; you try to fix a broken part or take it out. In Chinese medicine, the body is seen as a garden. If the leaves are wilting or turning brown, you examine the condition of the soil; see if the plant is getting enough water and sun, or if the roots are being impinged upon. You don't just paint the leaves green!" – "Between Heaven and Earth"

The Modern Western approach to medicine is "war on disease," with doctors as generals, disease as the enemy, patients as occupied territory, and the goal is to eradicate symptoms and maximize performance.

The Eastern approach (as well as many other worldviews) is to cultivate health with doctor and patient in partnership, to improve ecological conditions, where the goal is to enhance the self-regulatory capacity of the patient. Health in this model means integrity, adaptability, and continuity. This health is sustainable.

Ayurveda

Let's explore an alternate view of food, and essentially, lifestyle in general, as the worldview of Ayurveda is an inherently holistic one. The word "Ayur" means "life," and "Veda" means science, so it is essentially a science of life and offers a body of wisdom designed to help people achieve their full human potential.

The two guiding principles of Ayurveda are that the mind and body are inextricably connected and that nothing has more power to heal and transform the body than the mind. In Ayurveda, freedom from illness depends upon the expansion of awareness, the alignment of that awareness, and the extension of that alignment and awareness to the body. Meditation and purposeful breathwork are simple examples of practices that will achieve this end. During meditation, your heart rate and breathing slow down, your body decreases the production of cortisol and adrenaline, and your increase the production of neurotransmitters that enhance well-being, including serotonin, dopamine, oxytocin, and endorphins.

Ayurveda emphasizes the practice of eating as colorful a diet as possible, and to eat your food with awareness – be in the moment WITH the food as you eat it, be aware of it in your body, be purposeful about the eating of it. Ayurvedic principles suggest that a simple way of achieving balance in your diet is to include the six "tastes," of sweet, salty, sour, pungent, bitter, and astringent in each meal. Doing so will account for all major food groups and nutrients. Including all six tastes also helps to counteract cravings and overeating.

DIETARY CHANGES

In your quest to live a life of peace and happiness, free of unnecessary stress and constant worry, look no further than what you are nourishing your body with. Everyone knows that the things we eat and drink contribute to health factors such as obesity and heart disease, but the enormous amount of other ways diet affects physical and emotional health is far less common knowledge. You are familiar with the saying, "you are what you eat," and in this chapter, we will discuss in detail the ways in which diet affects stress levels, as well as the mechanism in which specific food and drink can help or hinder your fight against chronic stress and worry.

The first thing that needs to be explained is the ways being in a constant state of stress, and rush negatively affects our dietary choices. The examples I will give are what I feel most of us can relate to. Many people will tell you that they rely almost solely on coffee to get through the day. An enormous number of people readily consume coffee every morning to start their workday and eliminate the sluggishness associated with their hectic lifestyle. There is nothing wrong with enjoying a hot cup of coffee in the morning, as it is a nice pick me up and is actually associated with numerous health benefits. The problem lies however when a person continually consumes coffee throughout their entire day.

At this point, coffee becomes an unnecessary crutch. It is very well known that the caffeine in coffee is a potent stimulant that gives a pleasant boost of energy, and is the primary reason most people consume it. You may have wondered how this actually happens, so we will discuss this mechanism. There is a neurotransmitter in the brain called adenosine. When adenosine binds to specific receptors in the brain, it acts as a type of neuronal braking system, slowing neural activity and causing you to feel sleepy.

When caffeine enters the equation, however, it actually competes with adenosine for the same receptors in the brain. Once caffeine is bound to these receptors, it actually tricks them into thinking that adenosine has attached, but since there is not actually any adenosine present, you do not experience the sleepy, tired feeling associated with it. This doesn't present much of a problem when caffeine is consumed in moderation. The issue is that when a person is constantly consuming caffeine all day every day to try and cope with a stressful schedule, adenosine never gets the chance to do its job and neuronal activity is always running in high gear.

The neurons in the brain need the chance to wind down after extended periods of activity, and when this is not allowed, the body responds by releasing the combination of stress hormones we have already discussed. Therefore, constant consumption of caffeine will in time raise your stress level, ironically making the reason you are relying on it so heavily even worse.

Another negative result that comes constantly being subjected to a stressful, hectic schedule is skipping meals and forgetting to eat. While to some this may not seem like such a bad thing, less food meaning fewer calories and weight loss, this is not actually beneficial. However, the food we consume is what gives the body the necessary vitamins and nutrients that it needs to repair itself and function at an optimal level. Make no mistake, it is important to keep a number of calories consumed every to the appropriate amount, it is equally important that you are giving your body the fuel that it needs to function properly and help you maintain your productivity.

The most detrimental dietary habit that is often the product of being constantly in a rush and stressed out is inadequate water consumption. Statistics show that a whopping seventy-five percent of Americans suffer from chronic dehydration. With such a vast majority of the population experiencing this, we really don't ever seem to notice this is occurring. This spells trouble for the health of an individual, as proper hydration is absolutely vital for virtually all bodily functions.

While I am sure you have heard the news that water makes up seventy-five percent of the body, what is more, important to point out due to the topic of this book is that water makes up an even bigger component of the human brain, eighty-five percent! How in the world can we expect our brain to function properly, keep our stress hormones at an appropriate level and allow us to manage our daily schedules when we chronically deny it the main ingredient it is made of?

Studies have shown that being even slightly dehydrated actually elevates levels of cortisol in the human body, showing a DIRECT correlation between stress and dehydration. To stress (no pun intended) even further the importance of being properly hydrated, we should discuss a few of the other serious health risks associated with not consuming enough water. Depression can actually be linked to dehydration as well, since we mentioned the brain is made up of eighty-five percent water, when dehydrated the cells in the brain actually start to malfunction, leading to feelings of grogginess, fatigue, and depression.

You are far more prone to give in to those worrisome thoughts and stressors that you are facing when you aren't properly hydrated. Furthermore, being in a constant state of dehydration is strongly associated with increased blood pressure. When the brain senses a lack of water, it instructs the pituitary gland to secrete a hormone by the name of vasopressin. This hormone causes the blood vessels to constrict, thereby increasing blood pressure throughout the body.

To wrap up the importance of maintaining proper hydration, remember that our bodies don't actually have a system in place to store water. Therefore, it is very important that the schedule you maintain from day to day includes remembering to drink water! Now that we have talked about a few of the dietary impairments that often result from always being stressed out, worried, and in a rush, we will get to some of the ways in which a proper diet can manage your stress levels, and even get into the specific food choices you can utilize.

The next food on our list that you should try to consume in your diet helps alleviate some of the primary symptoms of stress, especially if you find yourself in a situation where you are face to face with a vampire (and not in the Twilight sense of the word). I am talking about garlic. While garlic gets a bad rap because of the lingering odor that comes with it, it can actually be a powerful stress-fighting tool. Garlic is bursting with antioxidants, like most of the foods on our list. It also contains allicin, which gives our immune system the jolt it needs when dealing with a stressful life. If you can get over the pungent smell associated with it, garlic is a good idea to try and make a regular part of your diet.

While consuming the fruits and vegetables that make up most of this list is always a great idea, it's time to add another protein source to our list of foods that will help you combat chronic stress and worry. Grass-fed beef is a great dietary option to help with this. Grass-fed beef is full of more antioxidants, vitamins, and essential nutrients than regular beef while having none of the hormones and antibiotics associated with the regular beef on the market.

This meat is one of the few dietary options, besides the fatty fish, we have already discussed that can provide you with a dose of Omega-3 fatty acids. As you have probably already noticed, grass-fed beef comes with a steeper price than traditional beef, but there is a reason for this. Grass-fed beef is better for the planet, as well as the chronically stressed out people populating it. If you can, spend a little extra next time that you buy beef, grass-fed beef will help keep your body performing at an optimal level, and mitigate the stress response that we are trying to avoid.

Our dietary friend, the cow, isn't done helping us alleviate stress and worry quite yet though. The milk they produce has recently been proven to pack a stress-reducing punch as well.

While the next food on our list our list is considered a delicacy for some people, and appalling to others (there really seems to be no in between), this food actually serves its role in lowering stress levels. I am talking about oysters! These shellfish are bursting with zinc, which actually reduces the secretion of cortisol during stressful situations. By no means am I suggesting you add oysters to your diet if you find them distasteful, any well-balanced diet should be one that enjoys as well.

However, if you are already a fan of them, keep up the good work! Oysters are truly a pearl when it comes to blocking the hormones that are released when you become stressed out. Milk contains a protein called lactium, which has been proven to not only lower blood pressure but also cause a reduction of blood pressure. Scientists actually began studying the stress-reducing qualities of milk when they noticed the calming effect it had to a baby after they fed on it. While you are hopefully getting your milk from a different source than the common infant, the concentration of lactium present in a glass of milk is a great option right before bed to help ward off chronic stress, as well as improve your quality of sleep due to the concentration of magnesium also contained in milk.

The food that we will now discuss is synonymous with being in a good mood and relaxation, and not even for the actual reason it helps with this. We are talking about turkey. Turkey is usually the centerpiece of everyone's Thanksgiving meal, a time when we are surrounded by our family and loved ones, being merry and enjoying each other's company while putting the stress and worry of everyday life aside for a little. It is unclear why turkey has become such the highlight of Thanksgiving dinner, but it was an excellent choice.

Turkey contains an amino acid called

tryptophan, which has a powerful ability to increase serotonin production in our brain. This surge in serotonin results in relaxation and mood enhancement. So in the same way that we should be thankful for our lives and loved all throughout the year instead of just on Thanksgiving day, try to consume turkey on a regular basis to fight chronic stress.

So far, I hope that this chapter has given you a general idea of the types of food and beverages to include in your everyday diet. It is of the utmost importance that we do not fail to neglect healthy food choices, no matter how stressful or hectic our schedule gets. When we do this, we actually compound the stress that we experience by failing to provide the mind and body with the vitamins and nutrients that it craves to continue running smoothly. The next and final piece of advice that I would like to give the reader isn't so much a dietary option as much as it is the method in which you prepare and eat the foods we have already discussed.

How often in the fast-paced rush of your everyday life do you actually have time to prepare yourself a nutritious, homemade meal, or for that matter get to sit down and enjoy it? When we are constantly on the run, eating foods that are pre-made, pre-cooked, and nutritionally scarce is a natural result of a frantic schedule. This is especially worse if you have a family to cook for and children to consider the nutritional needs of. You may think that there is no way you can provide them with a home-cooked, delicious meal all the time, but I'd like to suggest a method.

You may or may not have heard of meal prepping in advance, but this strategy is an excellent way to provide quality nutrition to you and your family, as well as provide several other stress-relieving benefits. Meal prepping is fairly simple, you talk with your family if you have one and make a list of all the foods they would like to have for breakfast, lunch, and dinner throughout the week.

Make sure these foods not only satisfy their taste buds but also their nutritional needs as well. After your list is made, travel to your local grocery store and stock up on the food you will prepare for the entire week. If you haven't noticed, you are making ONE trip to the grocery store per week. Not only does this free up time during your week from having to run back and pick up ingredients for dinner for the night, but it also eliminates running to your local drive-thru and filling the family up on fast food.

Additionally, making one voyage to the grocery store per week alleviates stress in a hurry by saving you money. One trip means less gas you spend to and from the store, and also reduces the amount of impulse buying that comes when you spend too long staring at that box of donut holes on your way to find some nice blueberries or grass-fed beef. After you have collected all of the ingredients for your weekly nutrition, I encourage you to set aside a few hours one day per week to become your meal prep time.

During this allocated time, cook and combine all of your meals for the week at once. This may sound like a lot of work, but after you get the hang of it becomes simple. I would also suggest investing a large collection of re-sealable containers in which to store individual meals in. Getting into the habit of meal prepping for the entire week in advance gives you several advantages for leading a more stress and worry free life throughout the week. First of all, preparing all your meals in advance eliminates the guesswork of what you will be eating every day, saving your time and brainpower for other important things.

Likewise, when you are able to simply go to the fridge, grab an individually prepared meal and go, this saves you so much time and energy and allows you to ease the strain of a busy schedule. You will spend far less money if you have a game plan for all of your meals in advance than if you are routinely going to a restaurant or convenience store to pick up a quick bite to eat, as anytime you have someone else prepare food for you, it is going to cost more than doing it yourself.

Finally, meal prepping for the week in advance can greatly reduce your stress levels and peace of mind by knowing that you are providing yourself and your family with nutritious, healthy meals that will allow the body to maintain optimal performance and keep that delicate balance of stress hormones where they need to be. The art of meal prepping is a great habit of falling into if you want to make consuming foods like the ones we have discussed in this chapter a regular part of your life.

In your mission to become a more stress and worry free individual, start by taking twenty-one days to evaluate your diet and the food choices you make. During this period of habit forming, reflect back on the foods and dietary methods we have discussed in this chapter, and do your own additional research if you have any more questions about how certain foods and ingredients play a role in your ability to combat chronic stress and worry. Before you know it, you will turn to these foods without even thinking about it!

Chapter 5: The Expansive Environment

"Perception is awareness shaped by belief. Beliefs "control" perception. Rewrite beliefs and you rewrite perception. Rewrite perception and you rewrite genes and behavior...I am free to change how I respond to the world, so as I change the way I see the world I change my genetic expression. We are not victims of our

genes. We are masters of our genetics." – Bruce
Lipton, Ph.D., cellular biologist

EPIGENETICS

Your genetic expression and development are shaped by your environment, and also by your reaction to your environment, and these changes can be passed down through generations.

On a social level, with regard to the environment, we are like sharks in fish tanks, in that the more expansive the environment, the more room we have to grow, the more growing we'll do and the more we will expand. This extends to the people you surround yourself with, the activities of your everyday life, your internal environment (food, thoughts, etc...) the extent of your ability to think critically, and your desire to evolve.

The more that we grow and expand, the more we positively affect ourselves, our relationships, and the world around us.

In a study by Chartrand and Bargh, researchers observed a phenomenon known as the "Chameleon Effect," which is the unconscious tendency to imitate the speech inflections, physical expressions, and body language of others in social interactions and interpersonal relationships, which researchers say can increase our likeability and make for smoother interactions. Perhaps this is the notion of "bonding" with regard to evolution and social instincts.

In the first experiment, seventy-eight individuals were asked to have a one-on-one talk with one of the researchers. Each of the researchers employed varying mannerisms - smiling, touching their faces, shaking their foot up and down, etc...

To determine whether the mannerisms had any notable effect on the interaction between the participants and the researchers, the participants were asked to participate in a second experiment in which they were sent to a room to converse with one of the researchers about a photograph. With half of the participants, the researchers maintained a neutral posture, and with the others, they mimicked their posture, movements, and mannerisms. Afterwards, the participants were asked to rate the likeability of the experimenter, and the smoothness of the interaction.

In the third experiment, researchers wanted to find out what kinds of psychological dispositions affect a person's tendency to engage in mimicry more than others. Researchers then evaluated the concept of "perspective-taking" or the degree to which people will adopt the perspectives of others.

Overall, the researchers found that the subjects whose mannerisms had been imitated had rated the researchers as more likeable, and reported having had smoother interactions with them. Additionally, the researchers found that the individuals who were more open-minded mimicked the face-rubbing gestures and foot shaking more often than others.

"Those who pay more attention mimic more, and make more friends in the process." - Chartrand

We are subject not only to the effect of others on our actions and reactions, but also our environment and the many subtleties, advertisements and subliminal messages clogging up our sensory perception. Having one foot in the awareness that you control your thoughts and desires, and another in the fact that you may be subject to environmental forces is a balanced practice. Perhaps that longing for black beans was the iron, but perhaps it was your unconscious noticing an advertisement associating black beans with happiness, success, sex, or youth. Becoming an expert in yourself allows you to expand your awareness of your patterns of thought and behavior, and recognize the various influences affecting your perceptions.

"When we become expert in something, our tastes grow more esoteric and complex. Becoming an expert in yourself, your observations will become more nuanced and complex, developing your intuition. Watch it surprise you." – Malcolm Gladwell, "Blink: The Power of Thinking Without Thinking"

"When you do not acknowledge how you really feel, you then subconsciously project onto others what you do not claim as your own." Becoming an expert in oneself, or in the art of "stalking" one's behavior, allows for a deeper awareness of motivations, patterns, and unconscious beliefs, allowing for a more expansive understanding of relationships and the ways in which we repeat unconscious behaviors until we are able to heal them by making them conscious.

What about your family environment and upbringing? How did that affect your unconscious programs? What beliefs did you acquire that you still hold? What are some that you've eradicated? What about our education system? What programs have we banked into our collective memory?

In the study "Enhanced Cognitive Flexibility in the Semi-nomadic Himba," researchers suggested that through formal education, Westerners are trained to depend on learned strategies, whereas the Himba people participate in formal education much less often, and were found to be more cognitively flexible, most likely due to a more unpredictable environment, coupled with the cognitive flexibility that comes not having been boxed in the first place. Cognitive flexibility leads to more innovative approaches and is a useful creative practice. Question everything that you know. What have you specialized in? What did you know about your practice before you were a specialist? How creative were you with regard to your practice prior to your study of it? In which ways may formal education "imprison" the creative force? How does the predictability and stability of our modern environment contribute to cognitive and creative atrophy? What can you do to spice up your environment? Your routine? Your input and output? Your thoughts and perceptions?

What about your views on the concepts of

"illness" and "wellness?"

What does health mean for you?

Chapter 6: Illness and Wellness

GLOBAL PERSPECTIVES

Have you read the book or watched the documentary "Horse Boy?" It's about a boy named Rowan who was diagnosed with extreme autism at a young age. Rowan's symptoms ranged from unexpected temper tantrums to isolation, difficulty in communication, and delayed cognitive skills. Rowan, however, found a haven in animals, and most especially horses, with whom he deeply connected. Rowan's parents had tried every kind of treatment for Rowan but hadn't had any success. Rupert, Rowan's father, who had spent some time living with the Bushmen in South Africa and had experienced their Shamanic healing powers, had researched Mongolian shamanism, and the culture of horses there, and convinced his wife to bring Rowan to Mongolia on a healing journey.

"It was just a short journey to the mountain, where nine shamans were waiting to meet us in a vast expanse of grassland. Some of the shamans were men, some women, and each was making their own preparations for the ceremony.

My doubts and fears rose to the surface again when Tulga, our English-speaking guide, introduced me to the chairman of the shamans' association of Mongolia. The man standing in front of me had a crushing grip and smelled of vodka. Had I fallen into a nest of charlatans?

'He's not good with new people,' I whispered to Tulga as he directed me to lift Rowan across to another shaman. Whispering words of comfort to my son, I passed him to the healer - as much as you can 'pass' a kicking, screaming child.

But once in her arms, to my great surprise, he went suddenly still - until the shaman's assistant passed her spiritual mistress a bottle of vodka, from which she took a hearty pull, then without warning spat the liquid all over Rowan's face and body. The result was predictable.

'Gi-raffe!' shrieked Rowan, plucking random words from thin air. 'Gotta go ho-o-ome!'

The second shaman pulled out a harp and began to play a strange tune. Then there was more vodka spitting. Rowan screamed as though being tortured for a moment before instantly calming down again.

'Let's go see some more shamans!' he shouted. We came to four shamans standing in a line, whirling, drumming, entering their trance.

Rowan gave a deep, bubbly giggle, and at that moment I knew he was okay. Actually, not just OK - I knew he had embraced the situation and was, at some level, at peace with this crazy ceremony.

The next shaman we came to whirled, sang and drummed as energetically as the others had, but whenever he came close to Rowan, his movements became quieter - gentle and slow. My son gave another of those deep-throated giggles.

'He'll be fine,' said the shaman. 'Just do this once a year for the next three years. He'll be completely healed.'

When Tulga translated this, I felt my stomach lurch. Did I dare believe it?

Then something extraordinary happened. We'd now been at the foot of the Bogd Khan for about three hours, and the light was fading. Clouds were gathering; a wind was getting up.

An eagle which had watched the entire proceedings continued to negotiate the shared territory of its branch with two ravens. The long, blue silk scarves used by the shamans snaked out from the larch limbs on the wind.

'Hey, Rowan,' I said, going over to where he'd

been playing by one of the dung and incense-smoking altars. But Rowan took no notice, his attention absorbed by the arrival of another little boy - a Mongolian child in a baseball cap and shorts.

Suddenly, without warning, Rowan ran over to the boy and started hugging him, laughing and shouting and grabbing at the newcomer's cap. Caught between annoyance and acceptance, the little boy stood stiffly but acquiescing.

This was astonishing. Rowan never took the slightest interest in other children. He was the classic autistic 'parallel player', preferring to ignore other children while playing alongside them rather than actively engage.

'Mongolian brother!' said Rowan. The boy looked surprised. A little wary, but he let Rowan hug him once more.

'Mongolian brother!' Rowan said again. 'Come on, let's go to the river!' My wife Kristin and I looked at each other in amazement.

For the first time ever, Rowan was playing with another child. Tomoo, smiling now, made a gentle cut, which Rowan parried back. At a loss for words, Kristin and I gaped as Rowan and Tomoo chased each other, laughing."

Rupert Isaacson, "The Horse Boy: A Father's Miraculous Journey To Heal His Son"

What IS the worldview of shamen on the subject of "illness" and "wellness?" What about the eastern worldview of the integrative garden? What about the Western view?

We know that the Western view of illness and health is very much "machine-based," "attack and destroy invader" mentality, and if our bodies are micro-representations of the world, this view makes perfect North American sense, doesn't it? Where does all the government money go in the United States? War? The United States in ever engaged in a war on everything.

The Shamanic view of "mental illness" is that "mental illness" signals the birth of a healer. In the Shamanic view, Rowan was a Shaman.

"From American Indian shamanism to esoteric Judaism, this concept has dominated for millennia. As it has now become clear, western civilization is unique in history in its failure to recognize each human being as a subtle energy system in constant relationship to a vast sea of energies in the surrounding cosmos." - Dr. Edward Mann, sociologist

It is the western habit to define, generalize and compartmentalize, and health is no different.

Our oversight in deeming the body and mind separate is one that we must painstakingly unlearn and correct if we want to evolve with efficiency in our understanding of the human being.

What do illness and wellness mean for you? Perhaps the words "ease" and "dis-ease" paint a more apt picture? What is a mental illness? The definition and the concept of mental illness has changed and evolved in the west and continues to do so as we learn more about the mind, the body, and the connection between the two, and will continue to evolve as we reach out and embrace other worldviews of illness and wellness.

"When conscious life is characterized by one-sidedness and false attitudes, primordial healing images are activated - one might say instinctively - and come to light in the dreams of individuals and the visions of artists.... schizophrenia is a condition in which the dream takes the place of reality." - Carl Jung

It is undeniable that with the explosion of the bodymind concept in the 21st century, ideas regarding illness and health will transform as medical thinking becomes more patient-centered, organic, and holistic.

HEALING ONESELF

Anything and everything that has ever been conceived of has been conceived of from nothing. Theories, medical practices, martial arts, concepts... anything that is, wasn't, at one time. What does that mean? That means that individuals and groups daring enough to follow their instincts and their intuition are the people that have conceived of anything and everything that humanity has ever done or been.

Why should you be any different? Do you need someone else's permission before you make your decisions? Do you need society to agree first before coming to your own conclusions about you, your body, your mind, your soul and your potential?

Moshe Feldenkrais first injured his knee while playing soccer, and then re-injured it while working slippery submarine decks as a naval scientist during the Second World War. Feldenkrais was also a Judo teacher and had mostly completed his Doctor of Science, and as the prospect of surgery would leave him with a life-long limp, he decided to apply his knowledge of physics, engineering, and martial arts to an intensive study of his own movement habits.

Judo was a main influence on the Feldenkrais method, as it differentiates between rote exercise and attentive movement, "the methods of physical exercise in vogue… exert only the muscles without any other goal, and one needs much will to bind oneself unfailingly to one of these methods. Judo is very different, in that each movement has a specific goal which is reached after a precise and supple execution" – Feldenkrais

So essentially, Feldenkrais took his health into his own hands using his intuition, the knowledge at his disposal, the observation and awareness of his movement habits, and purposeful attention directed, at the moment, into and through his movements.

Feldenkrais also incorporated a variety of other schools of thought including "cybernetics," which is the "scientific study of control and communication in the animal and the machine," and is a transdisciplinary approach to exploring regulatory systems, their structures, constraints, and possibilities.

NOW WHAT

"The idea of victimage is a dreadful thing, a product of a safe middle-class perspective. What people who are not safe develop is tragic wisdom, the wisdom that embraces contradiction and seeks a sense of balance rather than going to extremes." - Gerald Vizenor

People all over the world and throughout the course of history have achieved the miraculous, pioneered new methods, and carved brave new frontiers in their decision to say "yes" to themselves, "yes" to their instincts and their calling, and "yes" to bold action and evolution. You are at the helm of your own dream, and no one can dream it but you. Gather yourself, gather your trophies and your understandings, gather your wounds and your tragedies, and use them to fuel your journey, to light your path, and to lift you higher. The journey through the dark night and to the dawn vanishes with the coming of the light, and in the glorious light of that proverbial morning, there only exists "right now," despite the lifetime that it took to reach that now.

You have the option, in every moment, to begin again at that moment. Every moment is new. Our bodies are ever in motion, changing over with the seasons, and intelligently evolving as we in turn service our own evolution. What if you could operate at your maximum potential?

What would that look like?

Throughout the course of this book, we've covered the waking dream, the mind-body connection, and the inherently holistic nature of health. We've explored the tales of neuroplasticity, and the experience of the miraculous, the power of an iron will be coupled with appropriate action, and the realm of the silent knowledge of the dreamer.

To be a dreamer, one must simply dare to dream.

ACTIVITIES, EXERCISES, AND IDEAS

Consider this portion of the book as a collection of topics discussed and subsequent supplementary or complementary activities.

Lucid Dreaming Technique:

WILD – "Wake-induced lucid dream"

- Lay down in your bed with your eyes closed
- Relax your body and mind completely (meditation is a good way to relax)
- Try to empty your mind
- Observe the state between waking and sleep, the "hypnagogia." Hypnagogic

hallucinations are vivid, dream-like sensations that can be potentially heard, seen, felt or smelled. Let your mind wander around and notice anything that appears while in that state, and "follow" it.
- Begin creating the dream scene
- Begin visualizing in detail and explore your surroundings
- Stabilize yourself within the dream often by reminding yourself that you are dreaming

WAYS TO REACH YOUR "INNER WELL"

- Be authentic
- Be brave
- Trust your process
- Follow your signs
- Focus on yourself, don't worry about what others are thinking or doing
- Feel without judgment

- Find a breathwork session or practice on your own
- Journaling
- Solitude
- Appropriate Sleep

PROBIOTIC FOODS

- Yogurt
- Kefir
- Sauerkraut
- Tempeh
- Kimchi
- Miso
- Kombucha
- Pickles

20 WAYS TO CHANGE YOUR MIND

- Believe that you can
- Align your language to your desires

- Live in the moment
- Honor your body by listening to it
- Dialogue with your body
- Meditation
- Intended breathing
- Gratitude
- Repetition
- Purposeful movement and action
- Adequate Sleep
- Take the journey to the bottom of your well
- Lucid Dreaming
- The art of stalking
- Visualization
- Physical Activity
- Eat well
- Commit to reducing stress
- Be mindful of the effects of your environment and make appropriate changes; shake up your routine and improve your cognitive flexibility

- Be committed to keeping an open mind

BUILD BETTER HABITS

If you ever hope to change your mind for the better it is vital that you change the negative habits that make it easier for you to stay just the way you are. Broadly speaking, if you feel better you will have a better outlook on life.

Self-discipline: When it comes to habits that ensure that you get things done, one of the most impressive is the ability to exercise self-discipline at will. While, as with most habits, getting started can be difficult, the following tips are sure to make the process far more manageable.

- Go all in: If you ever hope to improve your self-discipline, you are going to need to commit to the idea completely. Giving it a go while keeping one foot out the door will only lead you to shirking your discipline when it suits you, which is no true way to build a habit at all. Instead, you are going to want to commit to the idea fully and stay on top of your reactions to ensure that if they slip from the disciplined path, you are right there to ensure they get back in line. Making a decision to commit fully to the task at hand will go a long way towards silencing your inner critic. If you don't commit fully, you then ultimately run the risk of falling back into negative habits after months, or even years, and destroying all your hard work.

- Keep an eye out for triggers: When it comes to getting in the habit of practicing self-discipline, it is critical that you take the time early on to consider the types of things that commonly trigger you to lose control. Getting a better handle on your triggers will make it easier to understand the underlying habits they prop up, which will make it easier for you to avoid the whole affair in the future. While you might not be able to think of any triggers right away, if you keep the topic on your mind, then as you go through your week you should notice things that are more likely to stray from the chosen path.

- Removing triggers: Once you have managed to make a list of your triggers, the next thing you are going to want to do is everything in your power to ensure you remove them from your general line of sight until you have your habit of being self-disciplined down pat. While you will rarely be able to remove absolutely all the power a given trigger has, you should be able to lessen it significantly, with practice.

- Understand excuses: When it comes to exercising your self-discipline, especially in a scenario that will require significant time and energy to completely successfully, it is completely natural for your mind to come up with excuses as to why it makes sense to take the easy way out, some of them might even be rather believable. If you find yourself routinely putting off tasks because you are afraid to overexert yourself, due to the commitment of those around you, because you have too much on your plate or due to external factors then you might need to take another look at those activities and determine how important they really are too you.

While it can be easy to believe excuses that your mind puts out, especially when crying off is the easier option when these situations arrive it is important to look into your heart and determine the true reason for the delay. What's more, however, once you look, you need to act on what you see, looking is easy, acting requires self-discipline and will become easier with time.

If you find it difficult to ignore the part of your mind that likes to generate excuses, making deals with it might work early on until you have flexed your self-discipline a little more. For example, if you are looking to get into shape and are having a hard time getting up to exercise every morning you can make it easier to ignore the possible excuses you might have by giving yourself some form of reward on the days you do exercise. Over time, and once you begin to see real results, you will find that you need the extra motivation less and the excuses will naturally fade away. Remember, perseverance is key.

If you still find yourself giving into excuses, make

a concentrated effort to change the spin you are putting on the lies you are telling yourself. Instead of blaming failure on external factors, place the blame squarely at your own feet and tell yourself you are really crying off because you would rather do something easier, because you are scared, or even, simply because you are lazy. When other things don't work, confronting yourself with the blunt truth of the situation will often do the trick.

Change your routine: When building a lifestyle based on self-discipline the easiest was to assure that the new you hangs around for good, is to make sure that whatever you are trying to do (or not do as the case may be) you keep doing (or not) every day until new routines develop and eventually new habits form. Once new daily routines become a habit you can then focus your willpower in a new direction. When building a disciplined lifestyle, start with one facet of your life, turn new routines into habits and then move on to the next, before you know it you will be a whole new person.

Build new habits: When first asserting your will over your body, the conditions, the timing or anything else that you previously used as an excuse to keep you from doing whatever it is you knew needed doing, will make your new habit feel awkward and extremely difficult but the good news is that this is normal. This is simply what forming new habits feels like and there is no shortcut for it. The only thing that helps is knowing that it will get easier over time, just keep telling yourself that and it should help you through the rougher spots.

The easiest way to go about creating new habits is to mix up your routine to help avoid whatever triggers you may have that influence the negative behavior. Such urges are caused by the basal ganglia, a part of the brain that deals in memories, patterns, and emotions. The rational part of the brain which deals with making decisions is the prefrontal cortex and when an action becomes a habit it shifts from the second into the first. As such, changing your routine by inserting something new can trick the brain out of relying on the basal ganglia and force it to go back to using the prefrontal cortex.

- Set the right goals: While childhood days may have provided us with many ideas of the things we would like to accomplish in life, (becoming an astronaut, doctor, cowboy, to name a few select careers) the stages of late adolescence and adulthood tend to give the majority of people a drastically changed perspective. This, of course, isn't anyone's fault. The world just operates differently than most people think when they lack any informative worldly experience.

Again, this isn't any one person's fault, but rather it's everyone's. Almost every single person is trying to accomplish something, or get something, and so it stands to reason that at some point, two people with a common goal will try to get the same thing when there's really only enough for one of them – be it a job, or a romantic partner, or anything really. What the result of this tends to be, more often than not, is that the person with the least amount of dedication and self-discipline will fail while the other will attain the success that both originally pined for.

This isn't to suggest that a person – any person – couldn't accomplish these aforementioned goals if they really wanted to, it's just that usually, they are faced with the problem we discussed in the previous chapter: motivation. They have a starry-eyed view of the potential job or girl they've been crushing on, but they only see the end result. As if they time traveled, they picture themselves in the glorious career or with that beautiful woman, and they envision themselves accomplishing these things without really taking into account all of the dedication and focus that is a pre-requisite to get there in the first place.

Again, that initial spark could be seen as necessary, because without those starry-eyed young adults who dared to dream, our society would certainly collapse. We would find ourselves with a dangerous deficit of doctors, lawyers, and cowboys. But again, the only people who end up making it in those roles are the ones with self-discipline, because again, it isn't just about having the desire to do something; it's having the dedication to back that desire.

The reason that most people fail is that the goal

they choose is too broad. For example, setting a goal of being rich doesn't take into account that it is really only an umbrella term that won't actually get you any closer to your ultimate goal. Instead of saying you want to be rich, setting a goal to be successful at a well-paying profession, for example, ensures the same end result while at the same time providing you with a number of guideposts along the path to ensure you can tell when you are moving forward and when you are only treading water.

Reduce social anxiety: Everyone experiences some type of anxiety at one point in their lives. When you get up to speak in front of a group of people do you get a bit sweaty? Do you blush when you meet someone new and forget what to say? If your called on in class, do you feel nervous because everyone is looking at you? This is all situations that most people will face at some point and it is common to have the symptoms that I described. When you talk quiet and get nervous, do you blame it on your shyness? Shyness and social nervousness are quite normal. Overthinking and feeling nervous at a point in your life could be described as anxiety, but it does not mean that you suffer from social anxiety.

- Imagine yourself being successful in social situations: As hard as it may be to believe, imagining yourself getting better at social interactions can actually have a measurable effect on your performance in the real world, but only if you go about doing it in the right way.

To get started, you are going to want to imagine yourself in a place that you are very familiar with, where you are likely to run into individuals that you do not know terribly well, if at all. When you are imagining this place, you are going to want to really visualize it. Picture every nook and cranny, think about the smells and the sounds you would experience and generally do everything you can in order to put yourself into that space as completely as possible.

Once you have a setting in mind, the next thing you are going to want to do is to put yourself into the space. However, you are not going to want to inhabit the space in your body as you would if you were really there, you will want to put yourself into the space as though you were viewing yourself in the third person. This is an important step as it will give you a buffer between yourself and all of those negative feelings which creates the unproductive feedback loop you are trying to avoid. You will notice how much easier it is to practice in this way if you try doing the exercise from the first-person view.

Once you are in the imaginary space and settled in a location you would be likely to inhabit in real life, the next thing you will want to do is to bring in someone you would like to have a conversation with. Remember, this should be someone you don't know at all or that you only know in passing. The specifics don't matter as long as you tend to be anxious when trying to speak with them in real life. It is important to start with just one person as opposed to a group when you are just starting out as you don't want the conversation to jump around too much for reasons that will soon become obvious.

With that done you will want to go ahead and imagine having a conversation with that person. You are going to want to think through both sides of the conversations and make all the responses, both yours and the other person's as natural and realistic as possible. At first, you don't need to do anything more than play out the conversation as it would naturally occur and try to get a real flow going.

As you move through the conversation and come upon stumbling blocks that normally trip you up, pause the conversation, rewind and try again. Try out various responses and see how they land, then go back and try them again and again until you are happy with the alternatives you have chosen. Don't worry about how long it takes, or how many different tries are required until you get it right, this is just practice after all. Your goal with the conversation, and with every conversation in general, should be to eventually reach a point where you can address a topic that you are knowledgeable about to speak on at length or an aspect of the other person's life that you are genuinely interested to explore further.

Once you have successfully made it through an entire imagined dialogue, odds are you have now spent upwards of 30 minutes practicing genuine conversation, regardless of the fact that you were providing both sides of it. This exercise primes your brain to continue working on these types of problems in the background so that your brain will be more primed to utilize these types of neural pathways in the future. It will also help you to learn to push past the occasional awkward or suboptimal response and find a way to keep the conversation going under less than ideal conditions. Again, all without having to deal with difficulties inherent in practicing with a real person.

Once you make this type of practice a habit you will often find that conversations you've had in your head are now popping into your mind at random times without you even having to consciously bring them to the foreground. Once this happens you know you are on the right track. What's more, you will find that these types of positive mental conversations often replace the negative self-talk that likely popped up in this space beforehand.

The goal with this exercise is not to try and accurately predict what the other person is going to say in every situation, as that would be practically impossible. Rather, you should focus on making the conversation flow as smoothly as you can throughout. Once you have this activity down to a science, you are then ready to take the practice into the real world and start having productive conversations with strangers. While it is natural to apprehensive at this thought, armed with this exercise you will be astounded at how much easier to do so the experience becomes.

- Ask for feedback: It is important to improve your interpersonal skills when you are dealing with social anxiety, simply because the way you see yourself in these situations so rarely matches the way that other people perceive you in the same situation. As such, while it will most definitely be difficult, one of the best ways to improve is to ask for feedback from those you interact with. At first you can go ahead and ask for feedback from those who you are comfortable interacting with, but eventually, you are going to need to go out on a limb and ask people you are less familiar with what they think of your social skills.

This is obviously going to be a difficult thing to do, but getting the perspective of relative strangers on your social strengths and weaknesses can be a big wakeup call when it comes to aligning the way you see yourself in these situations and the way others see you. The easiest way to go about doing so is to find a group of people whose opinion you don't especially care about and then go to town. Again, it is going to be awkward, but the results are likely to surprise you. Unless you are doing something extremely wrong, odds are they won't have anything but praise, or at least, anything negative to say. As a general rule, people are far more critical of themselves than they are of other people.

Spend time around those with well-defined social skills: Another useful exercise is to spend time around people who have already spent time honing their social skills. Finding a local Toastmaster's club is a good place to start. These meetings are filled with people who are gregarious and enjoy spending time with other people. While this may seem like the last place you would want to go, the opposite is actually true.

First, you will be able to watch these types of people in their natural habitat, which can help you learn the mannerisms that stick out to you and allow you to file them away for future use. Additionally, if you spend a lot of time around these types of people you will be surprised to learn that you will start to pick up their habits and mannerisms without consciously thinking about them.

What's more, as these are the types of people who are naturally outgoing, you will likely find that it is much easier to get into a conversation with any one of them without having to try very hard. Likewise, you will most likely find that they will naturally carry the conversation along without you having to necessarily contribute much at all. This means it is a great way to get into the habit of having regular conversations with people without having to worry about doing it wrong or letting your hang-ups about social situations come into play. After all, these types of meetings are all about talking to people and learning to do so more effectively two things that you are already trying to master.

Chapter 7: How To Improve Brain Health With Meditation

Mindfulness meditation is a type of meditation which focuses on being as aware of each moment as possible, thereby helping the consciousness to expand by forming a stronger connection with the present. Mindfulness meditation has a long history of practice as part of the Buddhist faith where it is revered for its ability to improve both mental happiness and physical well-being. This has been corroborated by research which shows that mindfulness meditation is a beneficial treatment for a variety of mental conditions. What's more, it has also been shown to be effective when treating conditions including anxiety, stress and drug addiction.

Practicing mindfulness is a skill and like all skills can be improved with practice. To practice mindful meditation, you simply try and retain as much focus on the current moment as possible with the help of repetitive breathing and the information being relayed by the senses. Studies have shown that practicing mindfulness for just 15 minutes per day can lead to measurable results when it comes to reducing stress and improving a sense of self. This is caused in no small part by the positive effects mindfulness has on emotional regulation, attention span, and body awareness. What's more, neuroimaging results show that practicing mindfulness also helps the mind process information more effectively.

Research shows that practicing mindfulness regularly can improve brain health as well as function and starting young will ensure your brain retains more volume as you age. Those who regularly practice mindfulness will also find they have a thicker hippocampus and as a result, have an easier time learning and retaining more information. They will also notice that the part of the amygdala which controls fear, anxiety, and stress is less active. With all of these physical changes to the brain is it any wonder that those who practice mindfulness report a general increase in well-being and mood?

Beyond the physical changes, regularly practicing mindfulness has been shown to decrease instances of participant's minds getting stuck in negative thought patterns while at the same time increasing focus. This should not come as a surprise given the fact that a recent Johns Hopkins study found that regularly practicing mindfulness meditation is equally effective at treating depression, ADD and anxiety.

In addition to the physical changes that you are likely to experience when meditating regularly, regularly practicing mindfulness meditation will also help you to more easily free your mind from any negative thought patterns you might otherwise find yourself getting stuck on making it easier to focus on the positive instead. Mindfulness meditation is so effective at this task that a recent study out of Johns Hopkins University actually found that it is just as effective at treating anxiety, depression and attention deficit disorder as many of the leading medications specifically designed to do the same thing. Another recent study also showed students preparing to take the Graduate Records Examination, the most common test to obtain admission into graduate school, who practiced mindfulness meditation regularly prior to testing scored approximately 10 percent better than their less mindful peers.

With so many physical and mental benefits, is it any wonder that mindfulness meditation is revered by Buddhists all around the world? The practice has its roots in a type of structured meditation called vipassana which, when translated, refers to a mental state that promotes living in the moment while still being aware of how the present and the future intertwine. Those who master vipassana are said to more fully understand the universe as a whole as well as their place in it.

In order to reach a state of vipassana, practitioners strive for what is known as the three marks of existence: impermanence, non-self, and dissatisfaction, which together are believed to bring unity to all living things. Non-self refers to the idea of understanding the boundaries between the self and the physical world with the understanding that coming to terms with these boundaries make it easier to fully grasp the intricacies of both. Meanwhile, dissatisfaction refers to the innate desire to seek satisfaction from fleeting experiences and the inevitable feeling that losing these things creates. This leads to the idea of importance as only by accepting the temporary nature of life can true happiness and inner peace be found.

If you thought mindfulness only had a benefit on yourself, you were wrong! Mindfulness is a practical and strategic way to benefit the world around you, as well! This amazing technique allows you the opportunity to improve your world through several different ways.

First, when you are mindful, you are much less likely to engage in arguments or conflict with other people. When you do choose to engage in a conflict, you will be much more rational about your approach, and the situation will likely diffuse quickly. If it doesn't, you will recognize that no benefit is being drawn from the experience, and you will remove yourself from the situation. Mindful people are generally much less emotionally charged in a negative format than those who are not mindful. They are more likely to be able to handle anger and stresses strategically, which means that even their "opponent" will end the situation in a more calm and rational way. This may simply diffuse one set of bad emotions, or it could trickle and encourage the other person to go learn about mindfulness and practice being more peaceful and calm in their own lives. You never know!

Additionally, the more we are in sync with the world around us, the more we are going to experience value from the world, and give value to the world. We are more likely to notice people who are struggling, so we can offer help. We are more likely to experience the highest joy we possibly can, which truly is contagious! Many other people who experience your intoxicating joy are going to turn around and experience some of their own as a result!

Finally, people who are mindful are generally a lot more considerate of the Earth itself. They tend to take better care of the world around them through many measures, including but not limited to recycling, not littering, helping clean up after others, taking care of plants and animals, and more! Doing all of this contributes to the healthy production and growth of the planet, which means that you are assisting it in thriving and maintaining its health!

GETTING STARTED TIPS

1. Find the time! This is probably the most difficult part of meditation. Without time, we find it easy to make an excuse to skip meditating for the day. Don't. Meditation doesn't require leaving your home or any kind of special equipment. All you need is your time and some space.

2. Observe the moment. Mindfulness is not necessarily quieting the mind or finding an eternal state of calmness. The goal here is simple. We want to pay attention to the moment we are in without judging. When we judge a thought or something we may have done in the past, we tend to dwell on it. That isn't living in the moment and is

not conducive to mindful meditation. While this is easier said than done, it is a crucial step to mindful meditation. With practice, it will be easy to achieve. Be mindful of the moment, of your senses and your surroundings.

3. Ignore those pesky judgments. Take notice of the times you are passing judgment while practicing. Make note of them and move on.

4. Always come back to observation and the present moment. It is easy for our minds to get lost in thought. Mindfulness meditation is the art of bringing yourself back to the moment, over and over, as many times as it takes. Don't get discouraged. In the beginning, you will find your mind wanders a lot. Reel it back in and keep moving forward.

5. Be kind. Even if your mind does happen to wander, and it will don't be hard on yourself. It happens. Acknowledge whatever thoughts pop up, put them to the side and get back on track.

As you can see, the basics are quite simple. These are the things you need to remember on a daily basis while you are practicing. What's important is that you find the time to implement the basics every day. Mastering the basics will make it much simpler for you to dive into the deeper aspects of mindful meditation, which we will be discussing a little later on. Before we move on, let's address some common questions people have about mindfulness. It's important to realize there is plenty of room for learning by trial and error. What works for one person may not necessarily work for you.

STARTING OFF STRONG

Choose a set time and stick to it: As with any burgeoning habit, it is important that you create a routine for your mindfulness meditation and stay with it if you hope for the practice to stick. It typically takes 30 days for a new habit to take root in your daily schedule which is why it is important to commit fully to practicing mindfulness meditation if you ever want it to become part of your routine. Due to its low impact nature, nothing external is required, it is very easy for many people to make excuses to get out of meditating, especially if their daily schedule is already filled to bursting.

If you find yourself always coming up with an excuse to get out of meditating in the moment, you may find the following piece of advice particularly useful. "Practice mindfulness meditation for fifteen minutes every day unless, of course, you are extremely busy in which case you should practice for thirty minutes instead." Don't let the outside world intrude on your potential for inner peace, find a time each day that works for you and stick with it no matter what; in a month's time, you will be glad you did.

Get started by focusing on the moment: While the ultimate goal of mindfulness meditation is to quiet the mind in an effort to find a state of internal calm despite the hustle and bustle of the outside world, many people find it difficult to achieve this state right out of the gate. Instead, you will likely find it easier to start to supplant any thoughts you might have by focusing all of your attention on the signals that your senses are relaying to you to the exclusion of everything else. While you might not feel as though you are receiving much data on the physical world, especially if you are practicing in a quiet, temperate space, the truth of the matter is that your brain naturally filters out approximately eighty percent of everything it receives, you just need to get in the habit of tapping into it.

Over time, you will learn to tune out the thoughts you have regarding your everyday routines and instead tap directly into whatever it is that is going on around you. When you do so, it is important to process the information that your senses are providing you, while at the same time making a conscious effort to not pass judgment or dig too deeply into anything that crosses your mind. Judging results in additional thoughts, one way or another, which tend to lead to even more thoughts, until it is practically impossible for you to focus on the task at hand.

Remember, when it comes to mindfulness meditation, the goal is to get as close as you can manage to the moment as possible, which means ignoring everything else that is going on, with the exception of what your senses are providing you. To reach this state, you will start by focusing on your breathing, especially on the way the air feels as it enters and exits your lungs, along with the way it smells and tastes.

Once you have narrowed your focus to only this band of information, the next thing you are going to want to do is to start expanding your observations to include the other sensations your body might be experiencing at the time as well. With the top level of your mind temporarily cleared of all your immediate thoughts, you can then focus on going deeper into yourself in search of the point where you mind is content not creating any new thoughts and simply exists in a relaxed, peaceful state.

Avoid your thoughts: When you first begin practicing mindfulness, it is perfectly natural for your mind to constantly fill with thoughts rushing to fill the void left by your previous actions. This typically occurs because you have trained yourself over the years, whether you realize it or not, to constantly move from one thought to the next, in hopes of solving the latest major crisis. This is, of course, practically the polar opposite of what you are striving for with mindfulness which is why it is only natural for you to expect a bit of an adjustment period.

Each time you feel these thoughts encroaching on your state of peace, you are going to want to approach them in the right way to maximize your time spent in meditation. First and foremost, you are going to want to approach these errant thoughts in a way that is completely devoid of judgment. You are going to want to avoid judging each thought and also refrain from judging yourself for having them. If you find yourself being sidetracked by a specific thought all you need to do is to mentally set it aside, center yourself on the task at hand and then continue on as before.

Again, it is perfectly natural for this to be a process that is more difficult than it sounds, but you may find it useful to think of your stream of consciousness as a stream of bubbles instead. Each thought is then enclosed in its own bubble, floating by you at a distance. You will then want to let each bubble pass you by and then disappear once it is out of sight. Alternatively, you may find it help to think of your stream of consciousness as an actual stream with a dam on either side. You then just need to close up both dams and the stream will dry up until you are finished with the current exercise.

Persevere: In order to ensure that practicing mindfulness becomes a habit that you can stick with, it is important to start practicing it with the correct mindset from the start. Specifically, you are going to want to keep a reasonable level of expectations to make the day to day practice more manageable. Keep in mind that it is perfectly natural for your mind to wander and seek out thoughts, even after you have been practicing for a prolonged period of time. Perseverance is the key here as only by pushing through the moments of distraction will you be able to find the success you seek. Ultimately you are seeking the level of mental blankness that occurs in the instant you have been asked a question but before the answer has come to your mind, reaching this state in a repeatable fashion is the key to mindfulness success.

EVERYDAY PRACTICES

You now know how to start your own mindfulness meditation practice, but you might be wondering how you can bring mindfulness into your everyday life. You also may not be interested in adopting a meditation routine, but you can still bring mindfulness into your life with a few simple actions.

As you have learned, humans have a tendency to go on autopilot, and this happens more often during the normal everyday tasks we have to do. These are the moments when you need to become more mindful. You don't have to clear your mind of everything, just become aware of what you are doing, and notice how it feels. Here are some activities where you can become more mindful.

Brush your teeth: When you brush your teeth you probably don't think about what you're doing. You've been doing it for years and it's not that hard. You stare at your reflection and focus more on how your skin looks than what you are doing. You may even have to run through your house with the toothbrush sticking out of your mouth.

Instead, start thinking about the texture and taste of the toothpaste and brush. Think of how the brush feels as you move it in your mouth. Think of how the floor feels under feet and your arm feels as it moves. Be mindful as you brush each of your teeth.

Wash dishes: Most people have a dishwasher now, but when you have to wash dishes by hand you moan as you approach the sink because of the menial task. You robotically scrub, rinse, and dry; over, and over again.

Instead, notice how it feels. Feel the water on your hands. Notice how the scrubber feels when you rub it against the dishes. Notice the difference between how the dirty dishes feel and the clean dishes feel.

Stand in line: There are lots of times where you will find yourself standing in line; the grocery store, shopping mall, DMV, wherever. You stand there, trying not to make eye contact, and groaning about the time that it's taking.

Instead, start looking at things, noticing them. Notice what the area really looks like. Look at the people around you, don't stare, they may take offense to that. Notice the smells, hopefully, they are pleasant. Take advantage of this moment to notice your surrounds, and to become more aware.

TIPS FOR MINDFULNESS SUCCESS

Stay Mindful of Your Actions: Too easily can we fall into a routine with too many bad routines in it. This can range anything from eating out too many times a week because you don't want to spend the time to cook to buying things on impulse because "hey, I've got a few extra dollars, so what's the harm?" While spontaneity is not intrinsically a bad thing, making decisions without considering them first can lead to a lack of understanding of the consequences.

When making a decision, one that may lead to a habit down the road, stay in the present and consider it. If you don't think about something as you're doing it (like buying fast food for dinner four times a week) it will become a habit without you even realizing it.

It works for good habits, too. Yes, waking up early on a Sunday morning to run in the cold is difficult, but if you stay in the present and remind yourself why you want to run, you'll find it easier to drag yourself out of bed. If you don't stay aware of the present, you'll find yourself pulling the covers over your head and falling right back to sleep.

Here's the kicker: Staying present and mindful of the situation or decision at hand is also a habit you have to force yourself to learn. So stay mindful of staying mindful and the rest just may fall into place.

Mindfulness of Your Thoughts: Mindfulness doesn't only affect how you view your actions; it also impacts how you think about your own thinking.

It's important to reflect on your thoughts throughout the day to understand your mind better and to change any harmful habits you may have. If you find yourself having negative thoughts about your habits, staying mindful of these thoughts will help you identify them and change them before it harms your progress toward a healthier you.

Your own thoughts about your habits or progress toward a healthier you are self-fulfilling prophesies. That is, whatever you believe about yourself will eventually happen. It's important to stay positive about your progress and understand that you may not see results right away, but if you keep telling yourself that you are getting healthier, the results will come after.

If, on the other hand, you keep telling yourself that you won't get any healthier because you can't see the results right away, you'll be more likely to give up and then definitely won't see any results.

Once you've moved past your doubts, you can begin to visualize your desired outcome. If you want to lose ten pounds, constantly visualize yourself losing ten pounds to help you continue your routine. If you visualize yourself staying how you are, you won't make progress.

Your mind is a powerful tool, don't let it work against you to prevent you from achieving your goals. Use it to your advantage.

Make a Schedule and Stick to it: What makes a habit a habit is the fact that you do it constantly without thinking having to force yourself into starting it. The only way to do this is to create a daily (or weekly) schedule and to force yourself to stick to it. The more you stick to your schedule, the easier it will be for you to stick to your schedule.

With technology today, creating and sticking to a schedule has never been easier. Smartphones are perfect for creating a calendar with alarms to go off up to a day before your activity is planned, so you can have plenty of time to pump yourself up.

Some of the best advice I've ever been given is also the simplest in theory: Set an alarm for when you need to do something. When the alarm goes off, do the task without hesitation.

If you have an alarm set for your daily tasks

(waking up, going to work, cleaning the kitchen, mowing the lawn, homework, the list is limitless) and do that task as soon as the alarm goes off, you'll have a much easier time creating habits and keeping them. Like all things, it's easy to make an excuse for not doing it at the time, but if you force yourself to get up and do whatever your alarm says to do, you won't have time to consider all of the countless excuses not to do it.

Stick to Your Habits: Habits aren't formed after only one or two days. For the first few weeks, you're going to have to force yourself to do whatever you want to make into a habit. On most of those days, you probably will hate it, but it gets easier after that first struggle.

On average, it takes about 21 days for an individual task to become a habit. That's three weeks of doing something that, honestly, you probably won't enjoy too much to reach a point where you can stand it. It's hard and can suck, but if you remind yourself of your reasons for doing it and stick to the schedule, you'll get to the point where you can't live without your habit.

Once you form a habit over those three weeks of pushing yourself, you may not fully appreciate how easy the task becomes. You may still hate running in the morning because of how hard it can be to wake up early. But once you get a habit locked in place, you won't be able to go a day or two without it without feeling the negative effects of not doing it.

It comes down to one thing to form a habit: Tenacity. It's all about pushing yourself to continue a task even when it's difficult to make it a habit in your everyday life. The aforementioned tips and tricks are designed specifically to make being tenacious easier and, therefore, making forming and keeping habits easier.

Make it an intention to improve your overall consciousness: If you have the motivation to improve your state of awareness, you are already on the right path to success. Having an intention alone will help you to home in on finding new ways to raise your self-consciousness continuously.

Be truthful: When you speak the truth, you immediately raise your consciousness levels. People tend to be dishonest during times when their consciousness is at lower levels. Individuals with higher levels of awareness tend not to lie because they respect themselves and wish to be true to their overall being. This aids in assisting all sorts of relationships within our society to become more conscious in nature.

Live for your purpose: While you never know when or how you will discover your purpose in life, once you do find a spark, take care of that little glow of light so that in time it will help you grow a fire. Once you harbor your sense of worth and purpose, you are then more capable of sharing it with the world, which will continue to help you raise your sense of awareness.

Be conscious of your decisions: When you are avidly in control of the decisions you make, you unknowingly activate neural pathways within the brain that aid in promoting inner peace, calmness, and self-control. If you are allowing others to take control of the decisions you make, you are not fully conscious and are less able to take responsibility for your actions.

Be open-minded: Always being open-minded is an aspect of the overall process of becoming more aware. If you fail to accept the diversity that resides naturally in our societies, you are only inhibiting the world from giving you loads of unique opportunities. It also keeps you from being more aware of life. Being open-minded means being attentive enough to go out and try new things, such a new cuisine, exercise routines, and other such things.

Seek out higher intelligence: There are many opportunities that one can partake in to become more intelligent. No one is keenly smart in all aspects of their life, and there is always something new to learn. While some people are more emotionally intelligent, others have a higher I.Q. level. Enhancing any form of intelligence means that you must be consciously aware in order to pave the journey to expand your horizons.

Conclusion

Thanks for making it through to the end of **Rewire Your Mind**: *How To Change Your Mind To Live A Successful And Positive Life On Your Own Terms*, let's hope it was informative and able to provide you with all of the tools you need to achieve your goals, whatever it is that they may be. Just because you've finished this book doesn't mean there is nothing left to learn on the topic, and expanding your horizons is the only way to find the mastery you seek.

Now that you have made it to the end of this book, you hopefully have an understanding of how to get started improving your mindset for the better, as well as a strategy or two, or three, that you are anxious to try for the first time. Before you go ahead and start giving it your all, however, it is important that you have realistic expectations as to the level of success you should expect in the near future.

While it is perfectly true that some people experience serious success right out of the gate, it is an unfortunate fact of life that they are the exception rather than the rule. What this means is that you should expect to experience something of a learning curve, especially when you are first figuring out what works for you. This is perfectly normal, however, and if you persevere you will come out the other side better because of it. Instead of getting your hopes up to an unrealistic degree, you should think of your time spent working on yourself as a marathon rather than a sprint which means that slow and steady will win the race every single time.

Especially when you are first transitioning from fixed mindset to growth mindset, you might find yourself putting a lot of emphasis on speed. "How fast can I do this?" might be your thought, often. This is because fixed mindset people are more focused on the rewards than the process. If you want to have a growth mindset, you need to transition your emphasis from the reward to the growth itself. Focus on the growth. Instead, ask yourself "How much can I grow from this?" and "How can I maximize my growth from this experience?" When you do this, you successfully transition to a growth mindset and place your emphasis on the growth.

Reflection is the best time to recognize whether you are making the progress you want to make, or if you are not growing as much as you could be. Take time to reflect so that you can see how far you have come and where your strengths and weaknesses are. This is a great time to identify any fixed mindset patterns that are still existing within' you and work towards healing them.

The "ideal image" of whom people are supposed to be and what we are supposed to be like tends to be where fixed mindset and perfectionism are rooted. If you want to abandon fixed mindset and foster growth mindset, you need to be willing to abandon the ideal image and pay attention to whom you want to be and what your ideal sense of self is. Then, work towards the growth that will get you there.

Goals tend to be major motivators for growth mindset folks. If you are willing to embrace your goals and work towards them on a regular basis, then you can almost guarantee that you are going to learn new things. If you are not, you are not setting your goals high enough. You should be willing to set new goals and work towards them consistently. Every time you reach a goal, set a new one. Have a few on the go at any given time so that you consistently have something to work towards. If you do not know how many is enough, focus on working on one short-term goal, one mid-term goal and one long-term goal at all times. This ensures that you are regularly focusing on learning new things of all sizes.

While over time it will become easier and easier to have the discipline to follow through on a goal, no matter the roadblocks in your path, it is important to understand the distractions that stand between you and improving yourself. The advent of smartphones has trained many people to adhere to an instant gratification mindset which states that anything that is worth doing is going to be immediately entertaining. This is completely counterintuitive to a self-disciplined mindset which is focused on deferring short term rewards for greater rewards at a later date.

It is important to understand that when it comes to self-discipline you are not a beautiful and unique snowflake, everyone else, even those who are extremely successful, has all of the same urges and tasks fighting for their time. What makes them extremely successful is their ability to dedicate themselves to the task at hand when the situation requires it. Don't wait for inspiration to strike or let modern electronic distractions get in your way, have the self-discipline to put your goals first.

If you find yourself losing the battle with negative thinking and considering abandoning all you have fought so hard to achieve, it is important to remember how long it took for you to reach the point you currently find yourself in. This pattern indicates that it is irrational for you to expect changes to come about any more swiftly. During these times it is important to understand how far you have really come and the positive improvements you have already seen. Remember, the only time you should be cross without yourself about a lack of positive progress is when you let that one instant be the catalyst to let bad habits start to sneak back in.

Book 2:
Mind Hacking

How To Rewire Your Brain To Stop Overthinking, Create Better Habits and Realize Your Life Goals

Introduction

A few years ago, studies were released with an alarming set of data regarding human beings and technology and how that relationship is responsible for decreasing the average person's attention span to around 8 seconds. We've all heard similar statements in the media or in news articles about how technology is changing our brains, how we've become addicted to our phones, and how this affects one-on-one personal interaction.

This is just one of the many reasons why it has become necessary to essentially "reboot" our brains in order to clear away all that excess information with which we are inundated each and every day. There is actually a phrase associated with this—information overload. Information overload is a product of the fast-paced nonstop society we live in where every electronic device, billboard and building is covered in advertisements, questionable news stories, celebrity gossip, and an endless array of entertaining videos, quizzes, pictures, gifs, etc. It is impossible, unless one completely unplugs, to avoid this onslaught. Unfortunately, many of us are tied to our technology for various reasons, and setting aside our devices for more than several hours is something many can't handle without worrying about family, feeling anxiety about missing texts, or missing important communications from our bosses or clients.

As a result, many people are drug into the daily cyclone of information overload which leads to added stress, anxiety and lethargy at the end of the day. Though stress can come from a variety of other factors in our lives, technology and information overload is usually near the top of the list, whether we realize it or not.

Add to this pressure at work, family or relationship issues, fitting in time for friends and social obligations, and caring for children, and you begin to cultivate a perfect environment for too much stress that often leads to anxiety and even depression. Stress is also a contributing factor in many chronic diseases, including those which affect cardiovascular health. The pressure to keep up and be successful is compounded in our society by the social media we feed our brains every day which show people at their best, happiest and most successful on a daily basis. It is natural to look at people like this and feel that we are in some way not doing enough, not making enough money, not working out enough, not enough of *anything*. This is where the low self-esteem, anxiety and depression can sneak in. So, if the stress isn't getting to you, the constant barrage of media telling you to do better in nearly every aspect of your life surely will.

What are we supposed to do? Well, the response to the kind of society we live in today is reflected in the myriad strategies that have exploded onto the market place. Everything from yoga, dieting and exercise strategies to energy drinks, vitamins and motivational conferences have been marketed as a potential solution to everyone's problems. This product reduces stress, that product makes you feel good about yourself, this dress will make you feel more confident...the list is unending as marketers continue to find ways to convince you that if you just buy their products, all of your problems will go away. So why isn't everyone perfect, beautiful, happy and healthy?

The problem here is that people keep trying to improve on their perceived imperfections by buying material things meant to solve their problems. There is a reason the adage "you can't buy happiness" has been around for so long.

When people throw money at their problems, the problems don't actually go anywhere, they're just covered up. This is not solving, it's camouflaging. As soon as that product has run its course, the problem will remain right where it was before. I'm not saying taking your family out to the movies to decompress from a stressful week is incorrect. What I'm saying is that using this or other temporary fixes to run away from constant stress that is taking a toll on your body is not the best way to address it in a meaningful and long-lasting way.

All of these quick fixes are external. Marketers and advertisements are creating a desire within you for their products and services as an external source of peace, calm, and happiness. But therein lies the crux of the problem—these things can only come in true form from *within* ourselves, not from the outside.

Everyone has goals for their lives. That goal may simply be to figure out what makes you happy, what fulfills you, or what fills you with purpose. Nobody other than you can determine these personal goals, and nobody outside of yourself can make you realize them. Sure, people can give you advice and show you the way, but it will be up to you to get there and reach those goals for yourself. You can hire all the personal trainers in the world, but unless you do the work yourself, you won't be seeing those physical improvements you've always wanted.

Similarly, the strategies and tips offered in *Mind Hacking* will be up to you to implement and incorporate into your life. Happiness and joy are personal, meaningful experiences that can only come from within yourself. It is what you do and how you think that ultimately determines your long-term mindset for your life—no product can just hand it to you. This book will challenge you to look deep inside yourself to address the thought patterns that are holding you back.

In Chapter 1, we will look a little closer at mind hacking and what we actually mean when we use the term. How do you hack your own mind? Can you actually change your brain?

Next, in Chapter 2, we will dig in a little deeper into the science behind emotion and your brain, how the brain connects emotion with experience, and how this can dictate how you respond to similar experiences in the future. We will learn how your emotions translate to behavior in Chapter 3.

Chapter 4 will explain the scientifically proven phenomenon that is neuroplasticity. This concept is why it is absolutely possible for you to, literally, change your brain. We will discuss this phenomenon using specific examples, and you will learn how this can be applied in your own life.

In Chapter 5, we will address some of the most common afflictions in our modern-day society, including excessive worrying, overthinking and anxiety.

In Chapter 6, 7 and 8, you will learn step-by-step how to begin changing your brain through consistent, daily practice. You will first learn to identify your personal goals, remove the negative influence and clutter from your path, then take your first steps forward toward developing new habits and realizing your personal goals, whatever they may be. It is important to note that this step-by-step guide can be applied to pretty much any goal you have in life.

In Chapter 9, we will introduce some meditation techniques that have been proven to sharpen the mind and help focus you in on your goals. There is nothing better than a daily meditation to help the brain clear away extra information, repair and refocus.

Finally, in Chapter 10, we will go over 10 daily practices designed to further boost your chance at success through strengthening self-confidence. You must believe in yourself and your own capability in order to keep moving forward. We know you can do it, and we are excited to share this journey and the secrets to mind hacking with you. So, let's get started!

Chapter 1: What Is Mind Hacking?

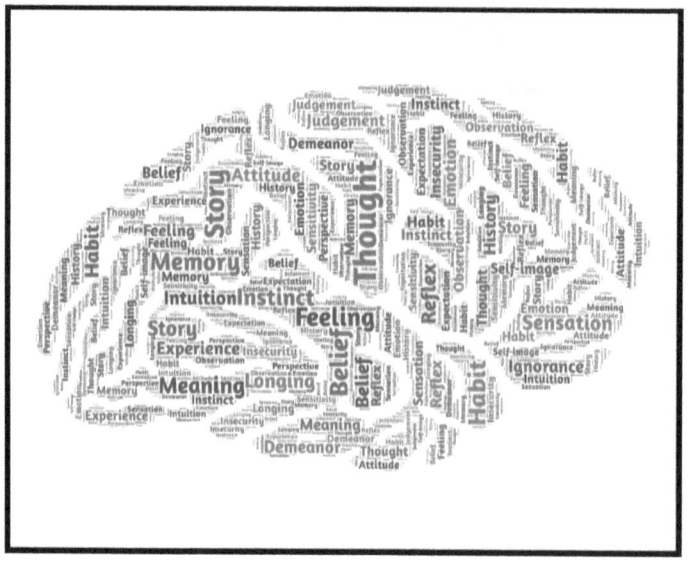

You've heard of hacking into a computer or hacking into a security system. Usually it's a smart protagonist or a criminal in a TV show whose fingers effortlessly move over the keys with a complex series of numbers on a computer screen before she hears a click or another sound to signify that she's been successful. So, what can we possibly mean when we talk about mind hacking? Is there a similar security system in place for which there is a magic code to get in? The analogy is an interesting starting point and has become a popular catch phrase in the media, but I'm going to explain to you what exactly I mean when I write mind hacking.

To do this, I'd like to illustrate with some examples of how the brain functions when it is allowed to simply "go with the flow" in our modern-day society.

Groupthink

A young man named Simon attends a staff meeting at work. He is part of a group of 7 people working together on a new software program for their tech company. The personalities of the people in the group vary. There are a few shyer individuals who tend to let others do the talking and prefer to work alone. There are a few individuals who actively participate in meetings and like group work. Then there is one man, Jim, who tends to take the lead in conversations. It seems to happen naturally, and he's not trying to take control from others. He is simply the most outspoken person on the team and very invested in his work. As a result, he usually has strong opinions about how to move forward on a project.

When he speaks, he uses a strong, loud voice that everyone can hear, and it sounds as though he really knows what he is talking about. When others in the group speak, they may feel just as strongly about their own opinions, but when it comes time to vote on a decision for how to move forward, Jim's plan usually wins. He's appealed to the basic tendencies of people to move toward those who display strength and leadership, even independently from what they think of this dominant person's words. Without thinking too deeply about Jim's words, the group is already immediately swayed toward him because of the conviction in his voice and the authority of his tone. Perhaps Simon introduced an opposing thought, but he spoke more quietly and less authoritatively. His idea may well have been something to consider for the project, but because he came off as less confident, the group gravitated toward Jim's ideas instead.

This is one example of a phenomenon called "groupthink," though groupthink encompasses a much wider arena of human behavior. Individuals moving together toward a singular, authoritative figure for the sake of harmony and group solidarity is a human tendency that has been around for thousands of years. A more familiar phrase you've probably heard many times is "peer pressure," which refers to the direct pressure one receives to behave the same way as the rest of a group. Peer pressure is very strong in the years of a person's adolescence because this is the time when he is trying to figure himself out and striving to find others with whom he can relate and experience this struggle. People will do a lot of surprising things for the sake of conformity and retention of status. It is hardwired into our brains to cultivate some kind of social status in order to be protected by the group. When you go against the grain and move in your own circle as opposed to others', you set yourself apart and become unimportant to those who choose to conform with their own. This was dangerous in the days when human survival depended on the strength of one's community as a unit for hunting, gathering and surviving.

The pressure to conform starts very early in life and continues throughout one's lifetime. A person will experience pressure from peers, family and authority figures insisting on exerting their influence on his/her behavior, thoughts, and belief systems. In addition, the person further experiences pressure to conform culturally through media and marketing efforts, as we've already discussed.

These influences have a much higher degree of success in winning over people who are not very self-aware. Some people simply do what they are told throughout their lifetimes. They may not spend very much time on who they really are, what is meaningful to them, or what their true belief systems are. They seem content to glide through life at someone else's direction, and these are the people who often make easy targets for those who wish to take advantage of their impressionable characteristics.

Cult mentality is also a good example of the phenomenon of groupthink at work. And it would be a mistake to think that only "weak-minded" people are susceptible to buying in to a cult or a cult leader's ideas. Victims who have spoken about their experiences talk of members who espouse a clear methodology when it comes to recruiting new followers, and their targets are weaknesses which are present in any human being who has experienced pain and adversity in some form. To demonstrate, think for a few seconds about a painful emotion that is connected to a memory. Something that has haunted you for years and which you've tried many times to run away or hide from. Now imagine someone coming up to you and sharing with you a similar experience she has had. Then, she tells you that she's found a way to permanently heal that wound and fully recover from that emotion. Would you keep listening?

Few of us wouldn't. Scam artists in many forms target and profit from their claims of being able to heal painful wounds. And this is just one reason why it is necessary to strengthen your mind, become self-aware and cultivate your inner confidence and conviction that you can change and mold your life according to your own personal goals; not anyone else's.

Do not adopt others' goals and ambitions for you if they are not what you believe would make you happy or fulfilled. It's hard to combat this influence if you haven't yet sat down and really thought about what these goals for your life actually are. Many figure it out too late, as they travel down a long road only to discover that they don't understand why they've come that way.

Mind Hacking Exercise #1

Mind hacking is about breaking free from the zombie-mode way of life. It is about stopping in your tracks, taking a look at yourself and your surroundings, and manually changing the trajectory of your life. A good starting point for you might be to think about and consider why you picked up this book. Why are you still reading? Has something you've read struck a chord within you? Does the scenario with Jim and Simon sound familiar to you? Do you also feel like you are following someone else's plan for your life?

Perhaps you've already discovered that there are things and thought patterns holding you back from progressing in your life in the way that you want. You are ready to proactively make a change and get rid of those habits and negative influences that keep you waking up stuck in the same spot every single day. Whatever your situation, I promise that by the end of this book, you will feel empowered and prepared to take hold of your own life and begin steering yourself toward the future you strive for.

So, let's find a good starting point for you before diving into the science behind emotions, behavior and neuroplasticity. It is important to feel oriented at the beginning of your journey before we move forward so that you don't feel lost or confused later. Set aside some time today to think about yourself and your life. I would strongly encourage writing down your thoughts in a journal and that you continue to record your thoughts and progress in this journal as you incorporate the strategies and tips in this book into your life.

First, think about or write down what it is in your life that makes you most happy. What makes you sad? Do you feel you spend a lot of time unhappy? How about anxious, depressed, or stressed out? Do you feel trapped, as if you have no choice in whether or not you feel these emotions? Before trying to move forward or adopt strategies, you have to understand where you are in life and why you are unhappy. Is there something missing from your life? Remember, happiness doesn't come from things, and it doesn't even necessarily come from other people. Happiness must be cultivated from within yourself. But perhaps there is something that you used to do as a child that made you happy that you no longer have time to do. Maybe you've really wanted to get involved with volunteering or a group that does weekly community service work as a way to give back. Perhaps you really just want to meet like-minded people who are in to the same hobbies and interests as you. Whatever it may be, now is the time to home in on the specifics and write them down.

Perhaps your happiness stems from the idea of removing some kind of negative influence or habit from your life. Perhaps you've tried for years to quit smoking and have been unsuccessful. Or maybe you have a friend who keeps encouraging you to be irresponsible and you think he/she might be a negative influence holding you back from achieving your goals. Write these down as well. In order to fully orient yourself, you must have the clearest picture possible of where you see yourself when you've achieved your life goals. You must also have a clear picture of the things which it might be time to let go of.

Don't worry about nailing all this down immediately. It will usually take a little time and reflection to come to terms with what needs to change in your life. As you discover new insight or come to decisions about where you want your life to go, write them down so that you can remember them and come back to them regularly.

Once you've gotten to this point, I'd like to introduce your first mind hacking exercise. Are you ready?

Find a quiet place to yourself where you are pretty sure you won't be interrupted. We're going to practice a simple form of mindfulness meditation to get you focusing in on where your thoughts tend to wander. All I want you to do first is observe your thoughts. Where does your mind automatically wander? Do you feel silly for trying the exercise? Maybe you keep thinking about something awkward that happened between you and a coworker almost a week ago now.

Now observe what kind of emotions you are feeling. Are they associated with some of these thoughts? Do you feel a wave of embarrassment when you think about something that happened at work recently? Do you feel residual anger from the traffic jam you had to suffer through on the way home from work? Don't push yourself to think of every single detail or to pinpoint your thoughts exactly and define them with emotions. Perhaps you are relatively calm and feel at peace just sitting and paying attention to your thought patterns. This is the idea.

Now, pay attention to your breathing. Breathe in for 5 seconds, hold for 5 seconds, then release the breath for 5 seconds. Don't try to push away your thoughts or think of "nothing." The idea is to simply take note of your breath and try to observe your breath for several seconds as you breathe in and out.

Congratulations! You've completed your first step toward hacking your mind. As we continue, you'll understand more about the significance of becoming self-aware as you create a new design for your life.

Chapter 2: Emotion and Your Brain

When we talk about emotion, most of us feel like we have a pretty good understanding of the concept. Emotion is what we feel when we are in love, and when we feel sad, angry, or afraid. These are kind of the big four categories of emotion that most of us think of, and most other nuances of emotion fall under one of these umbrellas. What you might not be familiar with is how exactly these emotions manifest in the body.

On the simplest level, our brains are constantly looking for two main things—danger and reward. When the brain detects danger, it sends out chemicals that make us respond. This is what's referred to as the "fight or flight" response. For example, if a person is out in the wild and they hear a sound that they've heard before in connection with a dangerous predatory animal, then he will become frightened. He will then choose between fighting and running away based on his knowledge and past experiences.

Most of us don't experience the exact same threat in modern-day life, but our brains still develop with this hardwiring that prompts us to respond in this way when we perceive danger. The brain releases what are called stress hormones—adrenalin and cortisol. These are responsible for the surge of energy we get when we are suddenly frightened. You may have heard stories about humans adopting a kind of super strength in times of acute stress. This is the adrenalin pumping through their bodies making them capable of dealing with the situation.

Similarly, when the brain detects a reward, it releases chemicals that make us feel good, including dopamine, oxytocin, and serotonin. These signal to the body to continue with whatever activity is activating the pleasure receptors. When we exercise, we get a rush of good feelings that encourages us to continue the activity regularly. Eating has a similar effect.

Modern Emotional Addiction

The trouble is that in today's world, we've come a long way from those times when the chemicals in our bodies signaled danger and pleasure to increase our chance for survival. Nowadays, most people on Earth don't have concerns in the same form and it is easy to abuse what makes us feel good. For example, eating is necessary for life, of course, but the brain can become addicted to the pleasure of eating food. Especially if we are eating unhealthy food, this addiction will start to affect other systems of the body and even deregulate the signal in our brains that signals fullness. When this happens, a person might overeat easily and not be able to tell when they are full, but the immediate pleasure remains the same. The response is deeply hardwired into our brains. Pizza and cookies will continue to initiate a pleasure response, even if we take them in at an unhealthy rate.

Illegal drugs form addictions in their users because they go right to these pleasure receptors and flood the body with pleasure. If a drug is injected, the effect is almost immediate. The person's need for the drug then escalates because he/she begins to need more and more of the drug to reach the same high as when they first started using. It is a vicious cycle and one that is very difficult to escape.

Did you know that we can also form addictions to our emotional responses? Let's look at some examples.

Do you know anyone who you would characterize as an "angry" person? Perhaps this is because he/she always seems to be in a bad mood when you see him/her. Or maybe you know someone who just seems to constantly be the victim of bad luck and is constantly whining about his life and the things that happen to him. The fact is, people can also become addicted to cycles of emotion.

To simplify this notion, think of the brain as being split into the "feeling" brain and the "thinking" brain. The feeling brain is in charge of these emotion responses to nuances of fear and pleasure. The thinking brain is in charge of our actual thought processes and reasoning. The fact is, the feeling brain kicks in quicker than the thinking brain, so it is easy to have an emotional reaction to an event before we can even rationalize what is happening. Let's examine the above examples a little further.

There is a man in your office named Sam who just always seems angry. He gets upset at the littlest incidences and seems to carry this emotion around with him all day. The anger response is triggering because he's trained his mind that this is the appropriate response to events which inconvenience him in some way. Now, it may have started out small, like getting stuck in traffic and being frustrated about it. But the longer Sam responds to things like a spilled cup of coffee, someone coming in late to work, missing a show on TV he was really excited about, having an argument with his wife, etc., with irrational frustration before engaging his thinking brain, the more his brain adopts this as the normal and expected response mechanism.

Let's imagine another man in the office whose name is Tim. Tim tends to come in to the office with his head downturned. He just always looks defeated in some way and is always complaining about things that happen to him on a daily basis. He feels the world and the people in it are just unfair and terrible and that he will never be able to improve his life. How did he get this way?

Well, he's formed an automatic response system to things in his life which he feels he cannot control. The process begins at the very beginning of the day and continues throughout the rest of the day until he is ready to go to bed. This is an extreme example, but the gist of the situation is that he's also taught his brain to respond with sadness and defeatism whenever something happens that sets him back in some way. These events could be as simple as getting a bit of his lunch on his shirt during his lunch break. His brain has been trained to respond with an overabundance of negative feelings about this, and thus Tim responds to the mishap as if someone had just run over his dog. He, too, has developed this emotional addiction over time as he continued to cultivate a general feeling of defeatism in response to the world. It has likely affected many other aspects of his character, like self-esteem and confidence.

Emotion can be an incredibly destructive thing if we let it form addictions in connection to our brain's response to life events because our brain also influences how we see others and their emotions. It's a strange phenomenon, but very true.

Let's imagine a woman named Valerie who experienced a traumatic breakup after her husband cheated on her in her early 20s. The experience prompted a serious depression and thereafter she's harbored an intense feeling of suspicion and dislike around men in general.

In this case, Valerie has connected her emotional experience with one man to all men she meets afterward, and this emotional response may continue for years and even for the rest of her life if it is not addressed. Her brain has made actual connections over time that link men and feelings of fear, anxiety and sadness, limiting the possibility that she will find a satisfying relationship with another man.

The influence of this emotional experience may go even further. To illustrate, let's imagine Valerie does finally meet someone with whom she's willing to try a new relationship. When Valerie is out in public with her new boyfriend, let's call him Zack, she reads things into his face that may not be accurate based on her past experience and assumption that all men are looking to cheat. If they pass an attractive woman on the street, Valerie may look over at Zack and believe she's seeing a look of desire on his face. When she confronts her new boyfriend about it, he denies that he was checking out this woman, much less desiring her right in front of Valerie. This is going to be very difficult for Valerie to accept because in her mind, she saw *with her own eyes*, the emotion of lust on his face.

Many people hold the assumption that emotion itself is connected in some way to a universal system of facial gestures and expressions, and this just isn't true. We may be able to make informed guesses about someone's emotions based on their facial expressions, but the truth is, the emotions we read in other people and on their faces largely come from inside our own brains, just like every other representation of our world. We all see this world differently.

Research has been done to demonstrate this phenomenon. People are given a picture of a man with what would generally be considered a completely flat affect and facial position. Volunteers are asked to fill out a survey about their own emotional states, past trauma, how they are feeling, etc., then they are asked to read the emotion on this person's face. What did they find? People's reaction and evaluation of the photo reflected the emotional states they'd reported on their self-evaluation forms. Those who had experienced recent trauma or sad events reported reading sadness in the face of the man in the photo. Those who reported a generally good attitude with no recent misfortune said they could see a hint of a grin on the man's face. Others reported anger or fear. The results are startling and tell us a great deal about our human tendency to "read in" to our daily lives and the people involved in them.

So, what does this mean for you? Are you trapped forever if you've found you have a vicious emotional addiction that pops up every time you hit a red traffic light? Well, I have good news.

Once we understand that our emotions tend to hijack our brains before our thinking minds can rationally respond, we can create a plan of action to slowly begin to adjust these emotional reactions. Research shows that we can absolutely influence our emotional responses through changing our thought processes, and this is part of what mind hacking is all about.

Interruption of Thought Patterns

The first step to address an adverse emotional addiction is understanding the emotional response. Where do you believe the emotion is rooted? Were you influenced by someone else in your life who tends to react a certain way? Perhaps you've experienced something traumatic that has influenced your outlook on life in general. Whatever the root cause, it is important to really think about why you react a certain way when it is something you very much want to change. It is the same principle as the prior exercises we did for discovering where your mind tends to focus throughout the day and writing down life goals. You can't start moving toward a goal without first having a clear idea of what it is, but also of what's blocking your progress.

I suggest you get out that journal again for this step in the process, as writing is usually a good way to really flesh out the detail of emotional responses. Write down your problem emotion and then write as much as you can about why it is you think you tend to respond that way, as well as why you think it is irrational. To be clear, we're not trying to eradicate sadness or fear or some other painful emotion from our lives. These emotions are relevant and incredibly important for a healthy human being. What we want to address are those cycles of emotions that do more harm than good and which we recognize as out of proportion with the stimuli. In other words, getting upset after stubbing your toe is reasonable; throwing your coffee thermos across the room every time someone does anything remotely annoying is probably not so reasonable!

I want you to look at your thoughts after you've finished outlining one adverse emotional cycle. Perhaps you have more than one, but don't overwhelm yourself. Focus in on one at a time.

Now, I want you to conjure an imaginary situation in your mind in which you are experiencing the opposite, positive emotion in opposition to this negative one. If you struggle with fear, imagine yourself in a situation where you are exuding bravery. If you struggle with anger, imagine yourself in a happy, stress-free situation, etc. Essentially, what we are doing here is finding a thought pattern to counteract the ones which follow a negative emotion. So, if you feel a blow to your self-esteem every time you see that one woman at work who seems to have the perfect life, imagine yourself walking in to work confident and with a smile on your face. You've achieved certain goals in your life, and you are feeling good about it. This is your weapon, and you will need to take some time to visualize and feel the positive emotion that comes with this imaginary scene.

Now, the next time you feel that negative emotion being triggered, focus your mind on that positive, counteracting thought and see what happens. It may take some practice, but it is important to be patient with yourself. A habit is never easy to break, and it will take consistency and a dedication to the change. Over time, though, if you can implement this weapon in the majority of cases when your negative response usually takes over, you will see a change in your behavior and overall mood. This is because you are actually rewiring your brain to work differently in those situations. Don't take my word for it. Try for yourself. Keep a record of your progress in your journal so that you can look back and see how far you've come. This will serve as a strong source of confidence and motivation as you move forward.

I'd like you to try one more simple exercise that you can do anywhere you feel comfortable. This is an exercise I've seen many motivational speakers across the world use in their workshops to demonstrate the power of the mind over emotion. Find a private spot to conduct your experiment, or if you are feeling confident, try the exercise out at the park. It might work even better!

There is an additional element that works hand-in-hand with thought exercises when it comes to altering emotion and self-confidence, and that is physical movement and posture. Did you know that simply forcing yourself to smile even when you don't feel like it will raise your mood? Try it!

Sit down comfortably or stand up straight and look straight ahead. Now, without conjuring any specific thought pattern, simply move your mouth to form a big smile. Hold it there for a few seconds. How do you feel? Do you feel a change? Did you feel silly and start to laugh? Laughter is a very positive emotion, you know.

Now, let's conduct a posture experiment. Stand up straight wherever you are with your shoulders back. Think of a time in your life when you achieved a goal or accomplished something that was a really big deal to you. Something you consider one of the greatest achievements of your life so far. Now, raise your arms up in a victory pose with your arms making a "V" above your head and your hands forming fists. Hold this pose for a few seconds. How do you feel? Did your mood change at all? Do you feel more confident? Most people respond with a surprised look on their faces as they say, "yes!"

Now, see if you can hold this posture and alter your mood. Try your hardest to start feeling sad or to lower your confidence level. Hard to do, right? Our body posture has an influence over our emotions, just like active thinking does.

Assume the opposite position with your head downturned and your shoulders stooped. Think of a time when you failed miserably at something. This should bring down your mood slightly. When you try to change your confidence level in this pose, it is also very hard to do. Your posture is so suggestive over your brain that even when you try hard, it is difficult to feel confident and happy while holding this abysmal posture.

We've looked at all of these examples in order to illustrate the malleability of emotional response. You do have more control than you think, and you can change your thought patterns for the better. In the next chapter, we will look at how emotion translates into human behavior.

Chapter 3: How Emotion Translates to Behavior: The Good, the Bad and the Ugly

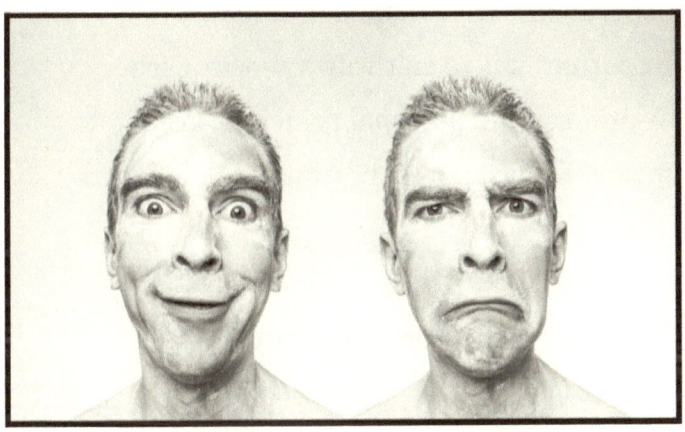

I n this chapter, we are going to look at a few of the most famous and controversial social experiments ever conducted in order to gain a better understanding of how emotions translate into behavior. The subheading of this chapter is, of course, taken from the classic Clint Eastwood film, and it will seem like we are mostly focusing on the bad and the ugly parts of human psychology, but we will end the chapter on a positive note. Just like we discussed in the last chapter, it is possible to rewire your brain to get off autopilot. These experiments have demonstrated just how important it is to cultivate a sense of self-awareness and personal principle, even if it means going against the grain of how others behave.

The Marshmallow Experiment

The marshmallow experiment was first conducted by experimenters at Stanford University in the early 70s and involved a group of young children. The children were brought in and asked to sit at a table with a big delicious-looking marshmallow sitting in front of them on a plate. The experimenter explained to the children that he was going to leave the room, and if the children could wait patiently a full 15 minutes without eating the marshmallow, they would get 2 marshmallows as a reward when he came back.

When the experimenter left the room, some of the children immediately picked up the marshmallow in front of them and ate. Others squirmed around and tried to wait but ended up eating the marshmallow just a few minutes later. Finally, a few of the children did manage to wait the full 15 minutes and receive the reward when the experimenter came back in the room.

This may not seem extraordinary by itself, but the most interesting discoveries were made long after the initial experiment. The children were observed from afar as they grew up and into their adulthoods. There ended up being an incredible connection between whether or not the child could wait to eat the marshmallow and the success they experienced later in life. Those who were willing to wait experienced more success in their lives than those who were not patient enough to wait before eating the marshmallows. The experiment offered a great deal of insight connecting patience and success over time.

The difference in these children was the natural propensity and capacity to understand effort in exchange for reward as well as patience. Being able to wait patiently allows one time to think through situations before acting too fast, and when this pattern of behavior is reinforced over time in the brain, it becomes natural and habitual to respond to situations by first pausing to think things through. Those who demonstrated a lack of patience and self-control were more susceptible to cultivating a pattern of behavior that allowed for acting first and thinking later. Without conscious effort to practice patience in life, a person is more likely to make rash decisions without thinking them through first. These individuals may also act on their emotions much more quickly and intensely, leading to unpleasant patterns of emotional triggers throughout one's lifetime.

Milgram Experiment

Let's move on to a much more disturbing and controversial social experiment conducted by a Yale professor in the early 60s. It is said that the experiment was born out of a curiosity that was prompted by a recent event in which a former Nazi defended himself and his actions in accordance with the Nazi party by saying that he was simply "following orders." This got Professor Milgram thinking. What actually happens when a person is put in a situation in which there is an authority figure applying pressure to follow orders in accordance with an established system or in harmony with others in a group of followers already following the orders? Out of this curiosity, Milgram created the now notorious Milgram experiment.

Subjects were brought into a room where a device was set up that was designed, they were told, to administer electric shocks at the flip of a switch. Another participant, whom the subject believed was also part of the experiment, was strapped in to a chair and connected to the device so that when someone flipped the switches on the other side of the wall, he would feel electric shocks equal to the number of volts above each switch…or so the subject believed.

What the subjects in the experiment did not realize was that the device designed to administer electric shocks was completely fake, as was the concept that flipping these switches would hurt the man strapped into the chair in the adjoining room. This man was an actor hired for the purposes of the experiment.

Subjects listened to their directions intently, though not without a bit of surprise and hesitation. The experimenter explained that the subject would sit in front of the electric shock device as the subject communicated with the other subject strapped in and connected to the device in the opposite room. He was to read off a problem for the man to solve. If the man answered the question correctly, nothing would happen. But if the man answered incorrectly, the volunteer was to administer an electric shock as punishment. Volunteers were told that the experiment was all about the utility of punishment in the process of learning and were unaware that they themselves were actually the real subjects of the study.

The study got interesting as the experimenter explained to the subjects that each time the man in the other room got an answer wrong, he was to up the voltage on the next electric shock administered. The volunteers were to go through a large list of questions and were asked to continue upping the voltage on the electric shock punishments. They were not given a limit or a point at which they should stop. At an interval of every few levels of voltage, there was a clear label identifying the voltage intensity, such as "minor shock" all the way to "danger severe shock," etc. The range of voltage went from 15 to 450 volts.

The questions Milgram wanted answered were: Just how far would people go? and why? The results were quite astounding.

As the volunteer sat down to begin, he would read off his questions and administer the shocks as prescribed when the "learner" got an answer wrong. This continued on up the scale of voltage until at a certain point, the learner began calling out in distress and pleading for the experiment to stop. He would yell things like "Let me out! Let me out! You can't hold me here!" Oftentimes, the "teacher" and subject of study would turn around to look at the experiment leader as if to ask, "Are you sure we need to continue?" Sometimes the subjects would verbally object to moving forward, but the experimenter would then apply a bit of pressure. He would say things like, "It is absolutely essential that we continue." After the statement, the experimenter would simply return to what he was doing with an absolute assumption that the experiment would continue. Faced with this pressure from a person they perceived as an authority figure and leader, a startling number of test subjects *actually continued* to lethal levels of shock. A whopping 65% of the participants, or two-thirds, actually went on until they'd administered the final shock of 450 volts. The *majority* of people who participated in this study were actually persuaded to kill another human being through what could be termed relatively minor authoritative pressure. What does this say about us as human beings?

We talked a bit about the ancient hardwiring in our brains in chapter 1 to maintain social status through adhering to social rules, often leading to the phenomenon of groupthink, when people gravitate toward the person exuding the highest authority. Similarly, the brain of the subject in this scenario is very quickly making decisions and forming associations which conform with what is comfortable and safe for them and their own status in the situation. The experimenter was seen as a strong authority figure with more knowledge and understanding of what was going on. In a position of doubt, the test subjects quickly identified themselves as the one with little understanding of the situation and deferred to the one in a position of power, knowledge and authority. Only in instances of extreme ethical opposition to the pain being inflicted on the learner were the test subjects able to stand up and withdraw from the experiment, their conscience outweighing their sense of self-preservation and appearances.

Out of these observations, Milgram and others who studied his work were able to analyze and postulate on how the emotional reactions in situations of intimidation, authority, peer pressure or all three at once influenced behavior. Human beings have an incredible capacity to rationalize and justify their behaviors out of fear or anxiety. Just as in the fight or flight response, the emotions triggered by the sense of impending danger essentially hijack the brain and prompt behaviors in advance of the thinking brain's assessment of the situation. Likewise, the threat of embarrassment or causing disappointment in the presence of a respected figure, and in conjunction with a very respected psychology department at a respected university, no less, was just too intimidating for participants to protest.

Perhaps this makes sense on this small-scale experiment level, but what about when we think about the atrocities committed by the Nazi party during World War II? Surely, no amount of peer pressure or authoritative influence is enough to justify the actions of those who participated in the Nazi atrocities, and that is absolutely correct. However, it would be a shame to ignore the scientifically relevant implications of this outrageous example of human behavior in the face of the Nazi party's influence. Much research and analysis points to a situation akin to the frog in a boiling pot of water analogy. If you've never heard of this analogy, I'm referring to the concept that you can actually set a frog to boil in a pot of water so gradually and so slowly that the frog will die without even realizing it was in danger. The frog adjusts its temperature according to the rising temperature of the water until just before boiling point, at which point it is unable to jump out because all its energy was given to adjusting to the water temperature.

Personal convictions, belief systems, and moral principles are all susceptible to outside influence and our emotional states. If we imagine a young man in the early stages of Nazi Germany, you have to understand the environment and atmosphere of the country and its attitude toward Adolf Hitler. Hitler portrayed himself as a very strong, confident leader, and his ideas about raising Germany up in status in the world was an alluring concept. We must see the gradualness of the change that would have taken place in those who became followers of the Nazi ideology as one idea is introduced at a time. After a while, a level of trust and confidence in one's leader is enough to feel an absolute sense of necessity to follow the leader's orders, even in situations where the individual may have previously questioned his actions.

A similar phenomenon happens within the cult mindset we discussed earlier in conjunction with groupthink. A conversion begins with a person latching on to one particular concept, then another idea that goes along with it, then another facet of the cult ideology. These ideas build upon one another, combined with an enthusiastic and charismatic leader, and soon you have a prior skeptic at home practicing cult rituals in the middle of nowhere as part of a notorious cult!

The Stanford Prison Experiment

Professor Philip Zimbardo's Stanford Prison Experiment from 1971 stands as perhaps one of the most outrageous and ethically questionable social experiments ever conducted. Nevertheless, we can't deny that the results of this prematurely halted experiment reflect a disturbing and fascinating part of human nature. The experiment truly altered the mental states and perspectives of the individuals involved, and to an alarming degree. Where there first had existed no great contrasts in general regarding socioeconomic status, disposition, or personal history, there soon appeared an alarming divide brought on by the simple introduction of power in a simulated scenario. One group of men were given the roles of the prisoners, and the others in the group were given the roles of prison guards. What followed over the next 6 days was truly extraordinary and was so notorious that a feature film was made depicting the incident in 2015.

A space inside the basement of a psychology department building was transformed into a small prison. There were bars on the cell windows and even a space set aside to serve as a place for solitary confinement, or "the hole." The guards were given "night sticks," sunglasses which covered the entirety of their eyes, and a uniform. The prisoners were brought in and were subject to strip searches before donning thin, flimsy prisoner garb for the duration of the experiment, which was to last two weeks.

On the first day of the experiment, nothing extraordinary happened. Everyone seemed to settle in to their roles with the knowledge that they were simply participating in an experiment.

The second day is when things started to get bumpy. The prisoners decided to rebel a little by barricading their doors with the beds they'd been assigned. The guards, in response, started to routinely punish the prisoners as a way to exert more authority over them. They'd been warned to do what they could to enforce order and maintain control, short of physical violence. Verbal abuse started to fly between prisoners and guards, and soon the divide between guard and prisoner was stark. Each of the individuals was starting to respond and take what was happening to them personally, and it seemed like they were gradually forgetting that they were participating in an experiment rather than a prison environment. One individual who was part of the prisoner group even decided that the experiment was too much for him, and he asked Zimbardo if he could leave. Zimbardo responded as a prison warden, explaining that he should consider staying and serving as an informant in exchange for better treatment. But the individual returned to the other prisoners with an understanding that he, in fact, was not allowed to leave, saying that no one else was going to be able to leave, either. Zimbardo maintains that he never told this individual he couldn't leave, but the prisoner had responded similarly to how a real prisoner would feel in this situation—powerless and at the mercy of the authority figures.

This perception fundamentally altered the experience for the prisoners, and relations between the two groups began to degrade further. Prisoners would be woken from their sleep to do disgusting chores, like cleaning toilets with their bare hands, and performing menial tasks and exercises. The process of degradation for the prisoners felt real, as did the feeling of power in the guards as they exercised their authority and control.

At one point, a prisoner who had disobeyed guards was punished by having him watch as his cellmates were punished for his behavior. They became angry with him, and the emotional stress had taken a toll to the extent that he asked to see the "warden" to ask to leave. Of course, Zimbardo told him he could leave, but down the hall he could hear his fellow cellmates chanting "Prisoner [prisoner number] did a bad thing!" over and over and over. In tears, this prisoner said that he couldn't leave and that he had to go back. He couldn't handle the other prisoners thinking he was a bad prisoner or a bad person. This really made Professor Zimbardo perk up because there had been this incredible transformation that had taken place within a short span of time. He had truly adopted this prisoner mentality, and what's more, he was feeling the pressure to conform within his own prisoner community. Zimbardo assured him, reminding him that it was only an experiment and that he wasn't a bad person or a bad prisoner. This helped clear his head, and the subject left the experiment.

The project escalated until a fellow psychiatry professor came to observe the experiment and ultimately convinced Zimbardo it was time to end it. Professor Zimbardo admits that he, too, fell into the mindset of playing the part of a prison warden and was caught up in the fascinating play of events happening before him.

The experiment was a game-changer, and subsequently there were guidelines and rules set in place to protect participants from experiencing such abuse and psychological pain as part of future experiments. But the harrowing results and implications remain and are still the subject of analysis and debate. The emotional feedback offered by power, in opposition to the emotional feedback in response to degradation, was powerful and long-lasting, according to participants who were interviewed after the fact. It speaks again to the susceptibility of everyday "normal" and ethical human beings to the influence of emotional response. Would the prisoners in the experiment have experienced such psychic pain had they continually reminded themselves that they were simply part of an experiment and that what was happening to them was not real?

Carlsberg Beer Experiment

I'd like to offer up one more example that may be a little more lighthearted to close this chapter on emotional influence on behavior.

As part of an ad campaign for Carlsberg beer, the company engineered a social experiment in which a theater for a movie playing one night would be completely filled with biker gang-looking guys, complete with leather jackets, gloves and beards…lots of beards. An unsuspecting couple would be led to the theater to watch the movie for which they'd just bought tickets, and they would enter a theater in which every seat was taken by these biker men except for two open seats right in the middle of the theater. Hidden cameras captured the reactions of these unsuspecting people. Some turned away as they associated these men with dangerous personalities and were uncomfortable. But those who simply walked up and took the two seats were rewarded with fanfare and free beer. (The looks on their faces are priceless, and you can view footage from the ad on YouTube.)

I want to take a moment to emphasize and augment the importance of the fact that, in the case of Milgram's study, there *were* participants whose consciences were able to help them rise above the influence of power and authority. It is not impossible for human beings to enforce their powers of logic and reasoning in the face of stress, fear, anger or other acute experience of emotion. It is far from impossible, in fact, and that's why you are reading this book. You know that you have the capacity and capability within you to rise above the groupthink, zombie-mode mindset which traps so many human beings for large portions of their lives.

Though the influence of society is strong, simply having a better understanding of human psychology arms you heavily to recognize situations in which you have a choice between unethical behavior in response to pressure or doing what you believe to be right or in your own best interest.

Chapter 4: Neuroplasticity and the Science Behind Forming Habits

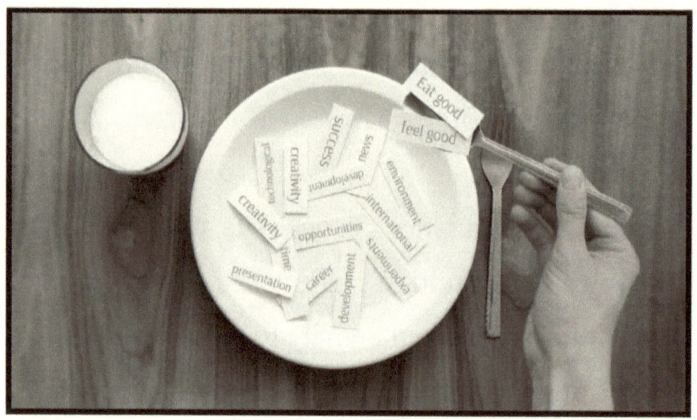

Within this chapter, we will discuss habits and the concept of neuroplasticity. If you've never heard of neuroplasticity, don't feel bad. It is actually a relatively recent area of study in neuroscience that has only developed on a large scale over the last few decades. Before we jump into how our understanding of the brain has changed in these recent years, let's take a look at some of the assumptions that scientists were working under only a few decades ago.

Like most areas of science, neuroscience has always been limited to the available technology and tools for gathering data about the brain at work. As a result, there were a lot of theories and hypotheses at work which relied on observation and the limited data that could be gathered at the time.

Scientists believed that the human brain was in a state of development until a certain point in young adulthood, at which point the brain was simply "done" changing. At this point, the brain had finished developing the essential components which make each one of us unique, like personality, disposition, demeanor, and certain thought processes. It was also believed that changing a person's habits became nearly impossible if the person waited until they were too old. It would prove to be a constant battle against the hard-wired brain connections if the person wanted to behave differently in some way.

Because of this way of thinking, people would resign themselves to the fact that after hitting a certain age, they would no longer be able to develop themselves into the vision they had for their lives. There was no real market for self-improvement, especially regarding things like mind hacking or fixing bad habits, because everyone believed that trying these things would be an impossible uphill battle. Children were pushed to learn things at a young age, and it is true that children have a much easier time of learning than adults in a lot of areas, such as language learning. It was considered essential for a child to learn the life skills and principles that he/she would need for the rest of his/her life as soon as possible. After all, they believed, "you can't teach an old dog new tricks."

But then the 21st century rolled along, and neuroscientists made some incredible discoveries.

The fact is, your brain does not stop developing in childhood or young adulthood. You have lots of neural connections in place, but it is possible to "rewire" the brain based on your conscious effort and thought processes.

So, what do I mean when I talk about neural connections and rewiring? Without getting too technical, let's explore the basics of neural connection in the brain.

Brain Structure and Habits

The basic unit of the human brain is called the neuron. The human brain contains over one hundred billion neurons. These neurons work together through their connections to other neurons to make things like emotions, feelings, decision-making, and an endless number of other brain activities possible. Each neuron is connected to up to a thousand other neurons, and these connections develop just like every other system of the body develops as we grow.

To illustrate, think of a young child who has just learned to walk her first steps. It feels unstable and scary at first. Her mother may be holding her hand as she places one foot in front of the other. But she's watched her parents and other people around her walk and has emulated other behaviors, and now she is ready to progress to walking. The brain is essentially taking its first steps in this regard, too. The brain is actively working to create a "neural network" that see her through the activity of walking. As she practices, her body adapts to this new practice; her legs get stronger, her balance improves, and her brain starts to memorize this pattern of movement and form the habit of walking until at some point, walking feels "natural" and easy.

As adults, we no longer have to consciously think about how to walk every time we want to take a step. That's because the neural connections in our brains are so strong from constant use that the roadway seeing us through this process is completely streamlined. The brain is amazing in that it not only makes connections based on what we are learning, but over time it develops a way to make the pathway faster and easier to access, like a road that was at first windy and full of holes that then gets paved, straightened out, then covered with oil for the fastest travel from point A to B possible. If you've heard the saying, "it's just like riding a bike," you already have a good idea of what I'm talking about, even if you didn't know it!

Riding a bike is generally a skill that we learn early in life, and the brain forms connections that allow us to not only learn the essential movements that go along with riding a bike, but also to strengthen those connections and improve on this skill. When you go for years without riding a bike, those connections weaken because they are not used as much. When a person first gets back on a bike after not having ridden for a decade or more, he may feel weird and off-balance at first. But the skill soon "comes back" as those old neural connections wake up and start firing again. You may not be as proficient at bike riding as you were when you were a kid, but if you decided to practice and ride your bike every day, you would find those skills coming right back to you.

These neural connections and neural networks are not just for learning basic life skills. When we adopt a behavior that later becomes what we call a "habit," we are basically describing a behavior which has become strengthened in the brain through repetition to the point that the brain automatically falls on this particular net of connections whenever they are triggered. Of course, there are many different habits, and the word sometimes intermingles with the term addiction. It is important to note that there is a big difference between a habit and an addiction. An addiction is often connected to a chemically supported impulse which the brain develops a need for in order to avoid the feelings that come with not getting that substance or whatever triggers the "feel good" chemicals that run through the body. Addiction does not always refer to substance abuse like drugs and alcohol; there are those who are addicted to social media, sex, food, etc., and these are connected to a release of those "feel good" chemicals we talked about previously when we discussed the definition of emotions. The alternative is for the brain to not release those chemicals and instead the person experiences symptoms of "withdrawal," which are never pleasant.

A habit, on the other hand, is a behavior supported by neural connections in the brain which is supported and strengthened over time. The brain has learned no other alternative to this way to accomplishing a task and has learned to default to this behavior. There are, of course, both good and bad habits. And there are numerous ways in which habit and addiction work together to form what seem like inescapable patterns of behavior. These in turn connect to certain emotional reactions, and you can see how difficult it can become when you decide you want to break free of this pattern of behavior when all of these forces are working together.

For example, take the smoker from the office who always goes outside to eat lunch, then walks over to the gazebo to have a smoke before coming back inside. There are elements of habit and addiction that overlap here to form a kind of expectation in his body that is nearly irresistible after years of conditioning this behavior and neural network of connections. When that clock on his desk hits noon, his brain kicks in to high gear, automatically associating this time of day with all the things he's conditioned it to. He will get up, he will go outside to the same picnic table. He eats his lunch, which might be one of a handful of usual lunches from his favorite restaurants nearby. Then, like clockwork, he wants a cigarette and goes to his favorite spot outside to alleviate this craving, releasing the usual chemicals into his body which signal that he has satisfied a very strong source of addiction.

In light of all this, it may seem like breaking bad habits and forming new ones is one of the most difficult things a human being could try to do, and sometimes it is. For some, it takes falling to an absolute low for them to wake up to the seriousness of their situation and how it is hurting them, emotionally, mentally, and even physically. For others, the revelation may be that they simply do not have enough good habits in their lives to get them to where they want to be emotionally, mentally, and/or physically. Each one of us is different with unique goals, habits, and life situations that must be addressed in the best way for each person. These unique facets of each human being who wants to change his/her life for the better will vary on a massive scale; but the universal truth is this—you *can* change your life, and neuroplasticity is a principle that every single person in the world can apply to do it.

Before we move on, I want to note that addiction is a serious issue, and the tips and strategies in this book may not be nearly enough to address such issues. Talk with close family and friends and consult your doctor if you feel you may need medical assistance to combat serious addictions.

Mind Hacking Exercise #2

This may seem like a lot of information, but I hope that you also find it as fascinating as I do. It's true that the human brain can be trained to throw a lot of obstacles at your feet when it comes time for you to change a bad habit or introduce a new healthy habit. But the brain is ready and willing to change according to your wishes. All it takes is a little effort and consistency on your part.

Get out that journal you've been keeping notes in (because, of course, you have been) and turn to the pages where you wrote down your progress for mind hacking exercise #1. In exercise #1, we practiced simply observing thought patterns as they came and went, noticing where our minds tended to wander and focusing on some of the things we tend to worry about throughout our days. Then, I had you write down your reflections as you watched these thoughts come and go, as well as record any emotions that are associated with specific thoughts. This may have seemed like a very simple exercise, but many people learn to run on autopilot, navigating their busy lives simply on force of habit without really thinking about what they are doing, where they are going, and whether or not that's really where they want to be. Remember, don't let anyone dictate your path for you. If there are facets of your life which feel like they've been running on autopilot, it's time to really look at these things and determine their usefulness in your life.

Review the things that you wrote down regarding exercise #1. It might be helpful to go through this exercise again if it's been a few days or even longer. See if anything has changed. What has remained the same?

Our next exercise is going to challenge you to experience the habitual brain in action. First, take out your journal and pen and write down a few things that come to mind in terms of daily mechanical habits. We're not talking about emotions or thought habits yet. What I mean when I say mechanical is something that you've trained your body to do each and every day without your conscious thought. Perhaps you walk the same way into your building at work, take a shower using the exact same sequence of movements, always hold your coffee mug with your fingers around the mug and looped through the handle instead of holding on to the handle, etc. Think of something like this for our little experiment. It doesn't have to be one of your big bad habits yet. We simply want to engage your brain and form a better understanding of neuroplasticity first. I believe having a solid foundation of understanding is important to a successful like-changing practice.

Your goal this week is going to be to adjust this mechanical habit slightly. Instead of holding your coffee mug the same way you always do, remind yourself to hold the mug a different way. Perhaps you will keep a sticky note on your monitor or something to help you remember.

The point of this exercise is to observe and record just how automatic these motor habits are and how difficult it is to adjust even the most menial element of the habit! See how you fare on the first day of this exercise. Did you need to constantly remind yourself to adjust your position? Was it easier than you expected? Did your body keep fighting to revert to the old way of doing things?

Write down your findings and continue the exercise each day for a week, or as long as you reasonably can if your days tend to vary. Keep track of your progress and especially at what point the task starts to feel easier. How long did it take for your body to start forming this new habit? Remember, every person is different, and everyone is going to form new habits at a different pace depending on the nature and intricacy of the neural network controlling that behavior. Just as with our first exercise, the real aim is to get you to simply observe these habits in action while also learning what it feels like to begin breaking a habit mentally. It may be a little frustrating at first, but keep at it.

Try to write at least a few words each day as you experiment. What is going through your mind? How does it feel when you redirect your mind to behave a different way? These emotions and mental pushback are going to come back when we dive into mind hacking more deeply to address bad habits and forming better ones, so take this time to get to know yourself and your own personal reactions. I promise, this will get easier as we go, and there are lots of things you can do to make it easier.

If you are having trouble with finding a good motor habit to address for this exercise, take a moment to look through this list and see if one of these might work for you:

- Walk in to the building where you work using a different door
- Brush your teeth starting from the opposite side of what you usually do

- Sit up in your chair with your back straight as much as possible (also a great healthy habit to continue practicing!)
- Use the opposite hand to use kitchen appliances, like punching in numbers on the microwave or setting the oven
- Sit in a different chair than usual during dinner time
- At the end of the day, kick your shoes off in a different area than usual (make sure it is ok with fellow housemates first)
- If you are usually a fast eater, try counting to five between bites during one meal a day.

Don't worry if it takes some effort just to get going with this exercise. If breaking and forming habits was easy, everyone would be in the greatest shape of their lives! Mind hacking is all about personal choice, willpower, motivation, vision, and strategy. You won't realize your goals without at least changing your mindset to one that will help you get there.

In the next chapter, we will address some of the things that often hold people back on their journeys to realizing a better way of living. We will discuss the various manifestations of anxiety and look at how overthinking and worrying affects people and their health over time. Harboring feelings of anxiety without addressing the source can really get in the way of your ability to move forward in life. We will discuss how to begin walking past these roadblocks so that you can move forward toward your new life. This step may prove more challenging than you think, but keep that vision of yourself at the end of your path, having reached your goals, to help you stay motivated.

Chapter 5: Letting Go of Worry, Overthinking, and Anxiety

We are all familiar with feelings of worry. As parents, we worry when our children go to school for the first time, when they begin hanging out with friends after school instead of coming home right away, when they start getting interesting in dating, and when they move out on their own. It is a natural tendency for people to worry about the wellbeing and safety of loved ones throughout one's life.

For many people, thought, there is a point at which worrying takes over rational thinking in situations where anxiety is heightened. They may begin to fear events or possibilities for which there is little evidence. To illustrate, think about the following scenario.

A young man named Sam is getting ready to complete three different college application essays. He has spent several weeks reviewing and researching universities around the US and their programs in his field of interest. He narrowed his choices down to three and then meticulously crafted his three essays according to each school's guidelines. He is a straight A student and has received much praise from his teachers who have also written him letters of recommendation. What in the world could he be worried about?

In today's modern world, young people are increasingly pressured to climb to the top of their competition and to stay there. Falling behind is unacceptable, especially for those who are more ambitious and capable. As the number of individuals competing for those top-tier jobs grows, the pressure to be the best is only increased further.

Pressure has a lot of influence when it comes to a person's emotional stability, especially in young people. A lot of people turn to look at each other in order to compare themselves with others. They do this to try to get a better idea of where they stand amongst the competition. Finding others "above" you in some way can feel like a crushing blow as a person scrambles to improve in their weakest areas in order to rise above.

We have to imagine that Sam has been tempted to look at how others in his own school are handling their senior years as they prepare for their own futures. Perhaps he begins to compare himself with others who have perhaps scored as good or better on entrance exams and standardized tests. Through this lens, his own personal academic weaknesses shine through and he begins to feel uneasy about whether or not these weaknesses will keep him from going as far as he wants to go in life.

It is easy for young people, especially those who are facing a milestone like this, to slip into the overthinking, constantly worrying mindset after they've begun looking around and comparing themselves to others. It is tempting to constantly use others' achievements as a measuring stick for how they are doing themselves. The minute we see others doing better, this starts to reflect on us emotionally and mentally, and this is why it can be so dangerous and self-destructive.

Sam starts to think every day about the possibility of not getting in to any of the colleges he wants to get in to, not finding the job he wants after he's graduated, finding out something is too tough for him and flunking out, etc. These thoughts, once rooted in our minds, can take hold and not let go. This is where the spiral down into anxiety can grow.

Overthinking happens when our worries and ruminations about future possibilities carry more weight than they should. Anxiety comes in to play when these outcomes tend toward being negative or what we perceive as failures on the part of ourselves or others. Anxiety tells us over and over that something has gone wrong in some way; you've embarrassed yourself, no one wants to talk to you, you'll never make the team, what if he meant something else by his remark? etc. These are just a few of the possible thoughts waiting to infiltrate our focused minds. Sam gradually loses sight of the fact that he is an amazing student with all the support of his teachers, friends and family and begins to see only the possible failures looming in his future. Hopefully, this is when someone from his support network steps in to reorient him and his mind so that he comes back to his former confident, capable mindset. But sometimes, this isn't so easy to do.

Many people move through life as fairly successful in their lives, both personal and professional, but also secretly carry very heavy loads of worrying, overthinking, and anxiety. It is not always apparent when someone is suffering like this because many people also feel the pressure to blend in and mask whenever they are struggling. No one wants to stand out as the person who "just can't handle it" and instead force themselves through experiences that actually take a great toll mentally and emotionally. I'm sure most of you are familiar with the concept of the workaholic; that student or coworker who always seems to take on way more than any one person should. These people may be feeling constant pressure to achieve more, do more, *be* more. As a result, they take on too much on a regular basis. Eventually, this person is likely to crash, most likely from fatigue. If he processes this experience as a failure, it may only fuel his need to get right back to his old routine. You can see how these thought patterns can quickly become destructive cycles.

The Role of News Media and Social Media in Perpetuating Anxiety

When occasional overthinking or worrying becomes chronic and self-destructive, it may earn the level of a genuine anxiety disorder.

There are many forms of anxiety which target different aspects of our characters and lives. One of the most influential sources of triggers for anxiety is the media.

Are you one of those people who simply cannot go a full two minutes without checking your phone for Facebook updates or text messages? If so, you are definitely not alone. Putting a discussion of social media addiction aside, let's focus in on the possible emotional ramifications of this addiction that may lead to chronic anxiety disorders. I've chosen this particular trigger because social media and phones are one of the fastest growing sources of addiction in our society today.

So, how exactly does news media and social media cultivate anxiety? Well, in the same way that Sam fell victim to comparing himself in terms of academic achievement, social media is a prime territory for people to begin overthinking themselves compared to others in a wide variety of areas. When you scroll through programs like Facebook, Twitter and Instagram, you see the faces of people and their lives. These depictions often make us feel as though we need to measure up in some way, and this need is propagated through marketing companies constantly showing us what we can achieve or earn or receive or look like if we only buy their products. This pressure combined with a constant barrage of perfect-looking, happy people is enough to fuel the anxieties of a whole generation and beyond. Eating disorders and self-esteem issues are at a record high in girls and young women. Girls as young as 9 years old begin thinking about dieting and getting thin like the models and celebrities they are constantly seeing. Men fall victim to the same pressure as well when they are constantly seeing images of the perfect male physique, which is usually accompanied by success, wealth and female companionship. These influences are not only strong but pervasive, and it is no wonder that a cycle of never feeling like you measure up can lead to chronic anxiety.

In the workplace, the constant pressure, both socially and professionally, is there to haunt adults of all ages. Those who grow older are constantly thinking of the threat of someone younger coming in to take their places. New, young professionals immediately start looking forward and measuring themselves against others who are going to be competing for the same rungs on the ladder in their careers. Everywhere you turn in life, there is another contest waiting to take hold of your mind. How can you ever break free?

Don't worry. There is hope!

Mind Hacking Exercise #3

Okay, it's time to get serious now. It's time to acknowledge those anxieties and thoughts that are holding you back and banish them forever from your life.

As always, you will need your journal or some paper or your tablet to take notes. This may be the most important exercise for you to spend time on before we move on to our step-by-step guide to rebuilding your mind. As I've stated previously, there is no sense in trying to cultivate new healthy habits before first addressing what is holding you back in life. You must clean away the clutter before filling your mind with new, positive energy and thought processes to transform your life.

Once again, you are going to have to put some mental effort into some self-examination. It's not always a pleasant experience, and we are going to be specifically targeting the nasty, negative anxieties and thoughts that circle over and over in your mind every day. You may be most acutely aware of this when you are lying in bed at night.

Many people experience sleep problems because they just can't shut off their brains at night. This is a common issue, as is reflected in the hundred of products being developed to help people go to sleep and stay asleep at night.

But very often, sleep medication is only camouflaging the issue, and there are definitive, effective steps you can take to improve your sleep quality.

The first step in this exercise is to write down the things you tend to worry about constantly throughout the day and at night before falling asleep. If you are one of those people who has a lot of trouble falling asleep, this may be your prime time for recording what you can't help worrying about. Are you thinking about money? What you have to get done at work the next day? That awkward comment you made to your spouse earlier at dinner? There are so many possibilities here. Your job is simply to take a day or two and really reflect on the things you tend to worry most about. Perhaps they are connected in some way, or perhaps it seems like a random mess of thoughts. This will become clearer as you take notes on your thought patterns.

Once you have a clearer idea of your triggers for overthinking and anxiety, we are going to engage a mental weapon in an effort to redirect the brain's wiring. You should now have a better understanding of how the brain forms networks to strengthen habits. Now it's time to start engaging this process to overcome worry and anxiety as much as possible.

First, focus in on just one of the items in your notes. It would be quite overwhelming to try to address more than one anxiety trigger at a time, so the key is to move slowly and really concentrate on the emotions that come with this particular anxiety you've chosen.

Take a moment to wrap your mind around everything this thought pattern entails. Is it connected with an emotion? Perhaps this thought makes you angry, worried, or sad. Whatever it is, try not to run away from it, but sit in it for a few minutes. What are the repercussions of this thought coming to fruition? Are these possibilities rooted in reality or is your mind running to the worst-case scenarios? Have you ever tried talking to someone you trust about this worry? What do you think would happen if you tried?

Now, once you've clearly enveloped yourself in this worry, it's time to construct your weapon.

I want you to carefully form a positive, counteracting thought that stands in direct opposition to your negative thought. If you are worried about next month's rent, conjure the scene in your mind of handing over a check to your landlord with the knowledge that you have plenty of money to cover the bill and to cover living expenses. Imagine the confidence and the happiness of fulfilling this obligation without financial concern.

Now, take a few minutes to sit in this scenario for a few minutes to wrap your mind around everything involved. How do you feel? What does the office look like? Are your children with you? Do you feel free, like a weight has been lifted from you? Form this scene in your mind with as much detail as possible. The more detail, including emotional detail, the better. This is your new weapon of choice for this thought.

The next time you feel something triggering this worry within you, redirect and interrupt the thought pattern by focusing in on your new confidence scene. Replace those old emotions with the ones you've just conjured and hold this feeling and scenario in your mind for as long as possible. It may be difficult at first, but the key is to practice consistently over time.

Record how you do during your first couple of days. Don't worry if it is quite difficult to train your mind. As we've discussed, breaking old habits and forming new ones is not something that happens overnight. Be sure to take note of when this process of thought interruption begins to feel more natural. It may take only a day or two, or it may take weeks. Each person is unique, and it's okay to be different or to take longer than somebody else.

Once you feel you have a handle on the process, move on to the next item on your list. It will probably prove too much to try to counter more than one thought process or trigger at a time. Give yourself time and take notes to keep track of how you are handling your new weapons. Perhaps you are having trouble getting over something awkward that happened at work between you and a coworker. The thought is accompanied by feelings of shame or embarrassment. You weapon may be the thought that you walk up to the person to have a conversation about the incident, and the person doesn't even remember it! All of your anxiety had been centered around this person's perception of you, so the idea that this person does not even remember what happened should go a long way to dissipate this feeling of embarrassment. Get the idea?

Take as much time as you need to in order to conquer those thoughts and feelings which may keep you from moving forward towards your new mindset. Consider recruiting friends or family you trust to help you along. They may have observed behaviors in you that you didn't even notice were happening as a stress response. Get to know yourself and your emotional pitfalls so that you can address them better. Try not to get defensive when you invite someone to talk with you and they bring up something they've noticed that they think you could fix about yourself. Changing yourself is about facing those things about you that you need to change. Don't get discouraged. It's all downhill once you've overcome all the roadblocks in your path. Your friends or family members may be able to help you dispel worries which were completely unfounded. Many times, people tend to conjure anxious or negative situations in their minds out of thin air based on others' experiences or things they are exposed to in the media. It is important to keep yourself grounded and not to fall victim to the scare tactics that often pervade not just news media but marketing campaigns. Fear can be just another way to get you to buy a product.

The next step in our journey takes us to a step-by-step guide to kickstart your journey towards a better you. The word "better" encompasses your health in every way, including mentally, physically, and emotionally. We will go through 3 chapters filled with the techniques and examples to accomplish the three things alluded to in each chapter title: First, we need to move our housecleaning mindset from the internal to the external as we identify outside influences which may be making it impossible to break free from bad habits. Second, you will create a detailed outline of what you want your life to look like. It's impossible to move toward a life goal if you don't have a clear picture of what that looks like in your life. Using similar visualization tools as introduced in this chapter, you will learn to practice seeing this reality each day to the point that it feels real in every way. Lastly, you will learn how to take one step at a time as you develop your new neural network based around self-improvement.

Chapter 6: Mind Hacking Step 1: Identify Negative Influences and Habits

The tools you learned in the last chapter are designed to help redirect your mind in the moment. As you use this tool over time, your brain will work to rewire itself until the point when you no longer are plagued by the vicious cycle of non-helpful thinking and instead defer to your place of confidence and self-worth. This is not a quick, easy process, and it will take time for the full and constant rewiring to take place. But rest assured, you've taken a huge step toward your personal goals by breaking the cycle of negative thinking.

This chapter is all about addressing the external roadblocks which may be lying in your path. Once again, you will need to break out your journal and something to write with. While the external influences holding you back may be more clear in your mind, they are often more difficult to address.

Before we get started on the writing exercise, I want you to go to a mirror somewhere inside your house. Once you are there, I want you to take a few seconds to look at yourself in the mirror. Focus in and observe the thoughts that go through your mind as you look back at yourself. How do you feel about your image? Are there things you wish to change? Are there things about your appearance you wish were different? What do you like best about your image? What have you come to terms with? Who do you most resemble? Think about how you feel in answer to these questions and any others that you can think of.

Oftentimes, when it comes to achieving our goals in life, the first and biggest obstacle is ourselves. What we think about ourselves, whether we have low or high self-esteem and self-confidence, how we present ourselves around others, or whether we tend to hide in the background. Your outside appearance and presentation is the first external obstacle you will need to address. Though feelings like confidence and self-esteem are very internal feelings, the way you present and carry yourself will have a big influence on your internal feelings. Remember the experiment where you altered your posture and observed your feelings changing? This is what I'm talking about. Even something as simple as making yourself smile will shift your attitude and confidence.

Try it now. Look at yourself and consciously adjust your posture. Keep your back straight and move your shoulders back. Use your thought interruption technique from last chapter if you start to point out things about your physical appearance that you don't like. These thoughts will never help you move forward. Instead, think of what makes you feel confident, your strengths and abilities, or your kindness and capacity for love and friendship. Whatever it is you are proud of about yourself, this is what you need to keep in mind as a weapon against self-doubt.

Hold this posture of confidence and put a smile on your face. This is where you want to be as often as possible—when you walk into a room at work or at a meeting, even walking into the grocery store. You can practice this attitude and posture wherever you go, and remember, the more you practice, the more you rewire your brain to assume the posture and attitude automatically.

Practice this in various surroundings until you feel more comfortable. As you do, get out that journal and write down how it makes you feel to adjust how you present yourself around others. What happens to your confidence in different surroundings? What is the hardest part about maintaining confidence? Anything that comes to mind as you reflect on this exercise, go ahead and write it out. Writing out your thoughts and feelings will help them become more clear. When you are ready, it is time to address possible negative influences coming from your relationships.

Addressing Negative Influences in Relationships

This may be the most difficult obstacle you have to surmount, or maybe you are lucky enough to only be surrounded by positive, uplifting people in your family and friendship circles. Each person's situation will vary greatly when it comes to how their relationships are affecting them, so, as always, we will begin with some writing to flesh out your own situation.

First, write down the people in your life with whom you are closest. The list could include lots of people or just a few. Anyone you can name whom you love and trust should be included.

Once you have your list, think about how each of these people affects you and how. If you have a partner, you may write a little bit about how this person makes you feel or supports you or respects you. Perhaps you write a little about how your mom or dad is always there when you have a problem or need to talk. This is your life and your list, so be as honest and open in your writing as possible. Part of addressing any possible negative influences in your life is acknowledging who you consider great influences in your life—these will include those who hold you up and support you in your decision to better yourself.

If you come to a person on this list and hesitate, you may have some things to think about in terms of whether the person holds you up or holds you back in some way. Now, don't get worried and think I'm asking you to cut ties with people you love. Sometimes it is as simple as having a conversation about how you need someone to support you instead of encouraging some kind of behavior. Perhaps you have a close friend who is always encouraging you to go out or drink or engage in some other activity that might not be best for you. Sit down and have a conversation with this person. Tell him or her that you are trying to conquer bad habits and develop a healthier, more successful mindset. You never know! You may just find a new partner to help you along the way. Perhaps someone on your list jumps out at you as someone who might also be interested in exploring ways to improve their lives and their mindsets. Be sure to open up and let them know how you really feel. If they are a true friend or a family member who loves and supports you, they will be willing to listen and adjust to help you. Letting yourself show a little vulnerability sends a strong signal to your loved ones that you trust them enough to open up.

Some of you will be in a more difficult position which involves a very clear negative influence in the form of a friend, family member or even your current partner whom you've been having second thoughts about. It is important to take some time to really think over how these people affect your life and what they offer you that is positive. If their negative influence over you outweighs the positive, then it may be time to seriously reconsider their presence in your life. Even family can be a negative influence if there is no shared love and respect. If you are not getting the support you need from a loved one, don't tie yourself to them just because they are part of your family. I've known many people who can attest to the fact that sometimes, it's friends who are the more positive presence in one's life, even above family. In the end, it's about who a person is inside, not necessarily whether or not you are connected by blood, which matters when it comes to living your life fully.

Whatever your situation, write down a thorough reflection next to each person's name and take note of those whom you think might be negative influences. The longer a person has been in your life, the harder it will be to think about leaving them. We as human beings love to maintain habits, and someone who is present in your life for years and years is no different from a habit that you've cultivated and grown attached to. It will be difficult to separate yourself, but if you've determined that the negative outweighs the positive, this might be essential for your life and your personal goals.

Determine who you need to talk to and set up a meeting. It is important that you do not go into the meeting with a hostile attitude. This person may not even realize the extent to which they've influenced you in a counterproductive way. The meeting should be about a conversation, not an argument. It will do you no good to get upset and start raising up your concerns as attacks. Prepare for the meeting by making a list of the things you want to address and the things you want to say. Perhaps it's not about turning this person from your life completely but asking them to step aside while you embark on a life-changing journey.

One more thing to consider before sitting down with this person is whether or not this negative influence is something that is also causing harm to your friend or loved one. If someone you love needs help with some issue, dropping a bomb like wanting to separate from them may be too much for them to handle at the moment. If someone you love is also a victim of negative influences in their life, this might be a good time to reach out and offer to help them conquer this negative presence together. Helping others forward can be a source of strength for your own journey and determination. Consider offering to share your experiences and tools with your friend or loved one as he/she battles his/her own demons.

Addressing Negative Lifestyle Habits

Another big obstacle in most people's lives comes down to personal lifestyle habits. We form them over time, and they are often influenced by society and those around us. They start early in life, and a lot of people never acknowledge that they may be cultivating habits that are keeping them from being healthy and productive.

Our lifestyle habits encompass everything from sleep schedule and eating habits to exercise and hygiene. Everything you do on a daily basis as part of your daily life and routine makes up your lifestyle. Yep, it's time to get out that journal again.

Turn to a new page and label it "lifestyle"

For this exercise, you will need to create labels under which to list your daily habits. Some essential labels will include "eating habits," "sleeping habits," and "exercise habits." You can create as many as you like, or else simply start listing off the things that you do every single day. Perhaps you are immediately aware as we start this exercise of some things which you should be doing but are not. These may include things like cleaning the bathroom and kitchen more often or taking the stairs instead of the elevator once in a while. Again, this is your personalized list and you can choose to address whatever habits you feel are most important to address. I would highly recommend the big three which I've listed for you above, as these will have a drastic impact on your health.

Let's walk through one of these categories together. Everyone has eating habits, so let's start there.

Under eating habits, think first about how regular and consistent your current eating habits are. In other words, do you usually eat your meals around the same time or are you always eating at different times every day? Describe this as thoroughly as you can. Are you someone who tends to skip breakfast and have a big lunch? Do you enjoy having snacks between lunch and dinner? Do you tend to keep snacking late into the night? All of these different observations will be helpful. Mindless eating is one of the easiest habits to fall in to and is something that has a big effect on our bodies over time. Or perhaps you are not eating enough and not getting the nutrition your body needs to function optimally. Writing down and getting to know your eating habits is the first step to pinpointing where you've gone wrong.

Next, describe what you usually eat throughout a given week. What are your favorite foods? Do you have a sweet tooth? Is there a restaurant that you frequent several times a week because it's convenient? Do you eat a lot of fast food? How often do you cook? etc.

The reason I like to start with eating habits as an example for weeding out negative influences and habits is because everyone is somewhat familiar with what a bad eating habit is and what a good eating habit is. You know that eating ice cream late into the night is a bad eating habit, and you also know that eating a balanced dinner that gives you all the nutrients your body needs is a good eating habit.

Once you have a pretty good list going, go back through and put a star next to the biggest bad habits you would like to change.

Now, write these starred items out again on a new line and create another column across next to it. You will now decide what better habit you need to replace the old, bad habit with. That's right. It's not enough to simply know what your bad habits are; now you need to decide why it's not good for you and make a decision about what you are going to do instead.

For example, if you wrote that you tend to eat a lot of fast food throughout the week, maybe 3 or 4 meals, then you might decide you are going to focus on meal planning and pack your lunches more often to make sure you are getting healthy food. If you eat a candy bar every single day and know you need to change this habit, write down that you should bring fruit or focus on passing on the candy bar at least one day out of the week when you would usually eat it. The idea is to get to know yourself and your habits as well as the things you want to change.

You next step is to write out why you would want to adjust these habits. What benefit would changing up that sugar habit offer for your health? How would drinking more water every day affect you? Why do you want to try learning to cook healthy meals instead of ordering out all the time? In the next chapter, we will focus on visualizing your goals and making them a reality in your mind before putting in to practice the steps you need to take to make them a reality for real.

Repeat this process for all of your big categories of lifestyle habits. You might follow up the eating habits category with a list of exercise habits. It has become much easier for people to lead sedentary lives because so many jobs require us to sit for long periods of time throughout the day. You may not realize it, but doing this actually has some profound effects on your health.

Start this category similar to how you started with the eating habits. Do you have any kind of regular exercise routine? What kind of exercise do you actually enjoy? What constitutes exercise in your mind? Keep going until you have a good idea of your exercise habits. Then, write out some things that you think constitute a healthy exercise routine as part of a healthy lifestyle.

What you may find surprising in regard to exercise is that, while many people in social media brag about completing difficult 1-hour or 2-hour routines every single day, you can actually drastically improve your health by making very small changes throughout your day.

For example, if you sit at a desk for long periods of time, simply making a point to get up and walk around every half hour to 1 hour will really help you counteract the adverse effects of sitting. You don't need to lift super heavy weights or run 10 miles every day to improve your health. As in an example mentioned above, simply taking the stairs instead of the elevator and taking longer walking routes to and from work will offer big rewards for your health. Introduce simple, equipment-free exercises at home like squats and lunges or sit-ups. These are all wonderful for muscle toning as well as good for your cardiovascular health.

Once you know what it is you need to improve, you can begin to create an idea in your head of what it will be like once you actually make those changes and realize your goals. In the next chapter, you will learn about the powerful impact of goal visualization.

Chapter 7: Mind Hacking Step 2: Set Your Goals and Learn to Visualize

You may remember several years back when a documentary called *The Secret* was released. The film was a huge success around the world. This film was all about something called "the law of attraction."

Researchers and interviewers dove deep into history to discover how different manifestations of the same law had been passed downed through generations but had remained cleverly hidden and set aside only for the rich and powerful, or those "in the know." The Secret claimed to be releasing this secret power for everyone all over the world to use. So, what exactly is the law of attraction all about?

The law of attraction is actually a quite simple concept to understand. The challenge comes when a person begins to incorporate it into their daily lives. I will explain.

When you want something in life, you think about it. Sometimes a great deal. Think back to when you were a child and the only thing in the world you really wanted was that BB gun or that bike or that basketball. I suppose nowadays kids are more focused on electronics than old fashioned toys like these, but you get the idea! When you're a kid, it seems like nothing else in the world would make you happier than that one thing. You include it on your birthday request list or your Christmas wish list. You do whatever you can to make it evident to your family and friends that you really want this thing. Then, lo and behold, Christmas comes around and you find your dream present under the tree. Feels good, right?

Visualize Your Goals

Let's bring this scenario up to scale and apply it to this concept of the law of attraction. The law of attraction tells us that we will naturally attract a scenario or object, or experience, or idea to us the more we concentrate our energy on it—or *visualize* it. It's really as simple as that. Now, for our purposes, we are concentrating on the visualization as part of your personal plan of action towards realizing your life goals. What this film dances around without quite saying it is that it is up to you to realize your dreams and take advantage of the opportunities that present themselves to move you closer to your goals. A million dollars isn't just going to float toward you if you dedicate three hours a day to visualizing money in your hands.

If you are interested in the unique angle on visualization and the law of attraction that The Secret proposes, it is readily available to you. This book offers a much more grounded and practical application to the concept of visualization. What we do know, through scientific research and data, is that your thoughts affect your behavior, your behavior affects your habits, and your habits determine your quality of life—that's all it comes down to. So, let's get to work.

Get out the list you prepared during the last chapter which outlined different facets of your daily lifestyle habits. We went over some possibilities having to do with eating and exercise habits, but I hope you were able to come up some personal categories for habits you would like to acknowledge and change. Remember that it's not about comparing yourself to others in your life. Their lives are not your own. You are unique, and you have something unique to offer the world. It is important to keep your goals practical and within the realm of possibility. Otherwise, you are simply leading yourself toward disappointment.

To demonstrate this process of goal setting and visualization, I'm going to introduce to you a fictional character named Laura.

Laura has been working for a tech company since she got out of college. She is a very smart woman and has done well with the company, earning the respect of both her coworkers and supervisors. After a few years, she starts to notice that the technology is rapidly changing and evolving, and she is struggling to keep up with new trainings that keep getting released. She is also noticing that positions are being taken up by new, younger professionals who are fresh out of college. They remind her of herself, though she has gotten a bit older. She begins to compare herself with these young professionals who seem completely up-to-date as far as the new technology and seem completely confident in their skills. There is a position opening up in a different department which is in a higher pay grade, and she has had her eyes on getting into this position for a long time. She talks to some friends and coworkers, and they all believe she should go for it.

She gets excited about going for this position, but as she continues to look at others in her own department, she starts to develop a habit of self-doubt. She no longer takes the lead in conversations during business meetings, and she doesn't seem to come up with as many good ideas for her group projects. Sometimes, she lies awake in bed at night wondering if she even deserves to be where she is, thought she's worked so hard to come so far.

Does anything about Laura's situation sound familiar to you? It's okay if not, I think we can still use this example as a good demonstration of how you can acknowledge your current situation, determine a better situation, then set and visualize goals.

Let's say Laura has a similar revelation one night and decides that she is ready to stop letting her negative thought cycles and bad habits get in the way of her success. What should she do first?

You're going to work through this process alongside Laura as a guide.

The first step is to create a list of concrete goals. The number of goals in your list could be as few as one or as many as fifty and beyond, whatever applies to your life. But we are only going to focus on one goal at a time, so I would suggest choosing one very important goal you can focus on and move toward right away.

Write down this goal in your journal. Now, I want you to explain in as few or as many words as you want why it is you want to achieve your chosen goal. This will help you nail down just how relevant and helpful this goal would be in your life. If the goal is superficial, you may find that your desire to achieve this goal is rooted in a place of anxiety or self-consciousness. Moving toward a goal for the sole purpose of alleviating an anxiety is something that you may want to look closely at. Wanting to lose weight because people at work have made rude comments toward you is activating a goal for the wrong reasons. This is why it is so important to not only home in on your goals but why you want to achieve them. Your goals should benefit you and your life in some positive way, not create as escape route away from the things or people who are hurting you. If you are being brought down by people at work for something like your weight, then the issue is not your weight—it is the rudeness and lack of professionalism displayed by your colleagues. If this conduct persists, it should be brought to the attention of someone who can take action to stop the behavior.

Laura's goal is to summon the courage and confidence to interview for the job of her dreams within her company. She wants to accomplish this goal because of the wealth of confidence it will give her, as well as the higher paycheck to provide for her family. She is also very happy with the work she does, and this position will afford her more control and opportunity within that field.

These are healthy reasons to want to achieve goals. They are not controlled by an adverse emotion and they benefit her not only on a material level but on an emotional and intellectual level as well. She hasn't chosen this goal to appease anyone or run away from an alternative choice out of fear. These are all signals that you can use as well to pinpoint the true motivations for your goals and whether or not they are truly long-lasting and integral sources of your future joy, confidence and fulfillment.

Once you feel solid in your choice of life goal, it is time to visualize yourself in a scenario in which you have been successful. We've practiced visualization in previous chapters as a way to combat negative thought cycles. Bring your skills for visualization into play here once again and turn your focus on this future joy in accomplishment. Let's walk through Laura's visualization for having accomplished her highest goal.

Laura sees herself waking up in the morning feeling refreshed and ready for her big interview. She gets dressed and feel confident as she heads to work. Maybe she's playing her favorite radio station or listening to her favorite podcast.

When she walks in the front door of her office building, she is greeted by the front desk and she responds with a warm smile. When it is time for her interview, her boss calls her into his office and invites her to sit down. She maintains great posture and a pleasant, confident demeanor as she answers each question pertaining to her readiness for this new position. She answers each question naturally and even throws in some humor here and there, which makes her boss laugh.

At the conclusion of the interview, her boss stands up and offers his hand for a handshake with a warm smile. Laura returns the gesture and thanks him for his time, then exits the office.

A few days later, Laura receives a phone call shortly after she's left work for the day. She is offered the job and will start the following Monday. Her face is beaming as she thanks her boss for the call and hangs up. Maybe she does a little victory dance outside her building and plays her favorite song from her phone on the way home.

The following Monday, she is escorted into her new office. She will get to decorate the area however she wants, and her office offers a new, wonderful view of the city from higher up in the building. Her boss comes in shortly to introduce her to some of her new coworkers as well as go over her initial job duties. Laura feels confident as she listens and nods her head as her boss goes over each step to the day.

Laura can close her eyes and visualize the moment when her boss comes in and congratulates her on her achievement. She imagines the weather outside, what she is wearing, how she's done her hair, and how others around her interact with her. Everyone is responding to her positive energy, and she seems to light up the rooms whenever she walks by.

This is an example of a visualization that turns a person's goal into reality within the mind. This is exactly what I'd like you to do with your own goal, no matter what it may be. It may be completely different from Laura's visualization, and that's fine. The reason I went through an example is to illustrate how much detail to give your own visualization. Really make it real in your mind with as much as you can add to the scenario.

Visualize New Habits Through Mindfulness Practice

Now it's time to revisit your top goal as you've written about it in your journal. You are going to create a new column next to where you've described this goal and why you want to achieve it. You task now is to list some new habits that you can work on to bring you closer to you chosen goal. Once again, we will use Laura and her goal as an example.

Laura has thoroughly imagined herself living out her dream of summoning confidence and courage to perform perfectly in a job interview and land the position she wants with in her company. Now that she can see herself clearly in this place, it is time to create a plan of action to start making this dream a reality.

What are some of the tools Laura will need in order to confidently conquer her self-doubt? Some of her healthy habits she'd like to pursue might include:

- Positive thinking and mindfulness on a day-to-day basis

- Daily mantra for confidence, sticky note reminders throughout the day
- Have one positive conversation with a coworker and/or supervisor each day
- Think of something to improve in terms of workflow and share with others
- Be proactive in meetings and brainstorm ideas to present for projects beforehand
- Practice being prepared for anything that comes up throughout the day
- Make time to work out every day or every other day
- Focus on a healthy lunch at least 4 out of 5 days of the work week
- Set aside time to do some extra research on the technology you're not confident with
- Ask questions and don't feel bad about having to do so

Laura's list could go on to include many more possible actions to take, but this is a good starting point. Notice that each of these courses of action move her closer to being prepared mentally and emotionally to complete her own challenge. She may focus on just one or two things at a time or try to tackle several at once as she incorporates them into her day. It is important that you take some time to really think through your action plan to determine which habits would be the best focus for you and your goal.

Create a similar list of items for your to focus on that will bring you closer to realizing your goal. In the next chapter, we will move on to how best to teach your brain to adopt these new habits, but one of the most important things you can adopt into your life is something called mindfulness, and we will discuss this concept briefly here before moving on.

Mindfulness is mentioned all over the place in conjunction with various spiritual practices, religions, and products. Mindfulness is actually a very simple concept that you can begin using in your daily life right away. It's all about paying attention to what is happening to you *here* and *now*. Too often people are worrying about or thinking about what's going to happen tomorrow, next week, or next year. They worry about what happened to them yesterday or last week and stress about what people think of them, etc. When we let our minds focus on things outside of the here and now, we really miss out on a great workout for our brains. Mindfulness has actually been shown to help the brain repair itself while clearing out all the clutter that is thrown at throughout the day in the form of information overload. We will get into mindfulness meditation in a few chapters, but what I want you to do is simply try to be more mindful of where you are in the present moment.

The practice is similar to how we created mental weapons against negative thought patterns. Instead of interrupting bad thoughts and introducing better thoughts, try interrupting your wandering mind and bringing it back to the present. The impact on your brain will be just as powerful as you are breaking down and forming a new habit, just like in our other exercises. It may seem simple, but practice over time leads to a huge difference in cognitive function, memory and overall mental acuity. You will also feel happier more often as you let the burden of overthinking lift from your shoulders. You will start to realize that a lot of what we all worry about on a day-to-day basis is ultimately useless and irrelevant. These thoughts can also become emotionally harmful, as we've demonstrated in past chapters. Protect your mind and fortify it for the tasks to come, because we are just getting started!

In the next chapter, we will zero in on a few of your healthy habit goals and learn how to slowly introduce the new habit into your life step-by-step. It may be helpful to see if you can recruit a friend to adopt a new healthy habit with you for support. You will find that once you've gotten the hang of how to slowly introduce change into your life, you will want to keep going as you begin to see the benefits of your new healthier lifestyle reflected in your body and mind.

Chapter 8: Mind Hacking Step 3: One Step at a Time

It's time to really get in to the nitty-gritty of changing those bad habits into good habits.

You should have some idea of the things you know you need to change in order to move closer to your goal. The idea here is to introduce one small change at a time and give yourself ample time for your brain to rewire itself according to that new habit. You want to concentrate on one small step that you will address every single day for three weeks. That's right—three weeks. Once you've developed this new habit, you will begin to build upon it by introducing a new habit for the next three weeks, and so on. You can choose to adopt just one habit to begin with, or you may feel confident that you can adopt a few different ones at once. It may be easiest to combine physical and mental habits so that you don't overwhelm yourself with a bunch of mechanical habits all at once. Remember our exercise with mechanical habits? It is difficult to retrain the brain to do something different from what it's been used to. That's why combining some kind of mental reinforcement with a physical habit is a good combination rather than trying to introduce several mental exercises into your daily life right away.

Once again, we can use Laura to demonstrate this process in action.

Taking her cues from the list we created in the last chapter, let's say Laura wants to focus on mindfulness and having one positive interaction with a coworker or supervisor every single day. The first thing Laura needs to do is prepare herself for the first day. She may already be familiar with mindfulness but watching some videos or reading some further instruction may be helpful. Her mindfulness practice will center around a 20-minute morning routine that will focus on her day, her goals, and her mindset. She may write out her own mantra to help her get started, and it might sound something like, "I will hold my head up when I enter work and keep a positive attitude throughout the day. Nothing can stop me from reaching my goals. I am strong. I am confident." Once she has prepared her mind, she is ready to tackler her day.

When she arrives at work, she may notice a supervisor walking past whom she hasn't had a real conversation with in a long time. Laura feels a little nervous about approaching her, but then conjures the courage to walk up to her.

She greets her supervisor and the greeting is returned warmly. Laura may find that the supervisor already knows a great deal about her and her ambitions. They talk for a while, and Laura maintains her positive attitude as she's promised herself she would do. When the conversation is over, she feels a wave of satisfaction and relief. She knows she is capable of conquering fears, and she sees that the key is to take small steps at a time.

So what about your own goals? It's time to choose one of your habits you want to adopt and begin making this change every day. Remember to choose according to what you feel comfortable taking on at first. You can add to your habits later. Perhaps you are determined to quit smoking and have decided to replace this behavior with something healthier, like doing some exercise during the times when you usually take a smoke break at work.

This is a good technique if your personal situation dictates that you need to replace one bad habit with one good habit. Sometimes simply focusing on breaking a bad habit is overwhelming without something to replace the behavior. Your brain needs something to fill the void and begin rewiring its response to the trigger. Some other examples might include: swapping water for pop, walking or biking to work instead of taking bus or driving, taking stairs instead of the elevator, packing a lunch a couple days a week instead of getting the same fast food you always get, greeting your boss with eye contact and a smile instead of a down-turned head, joining in on a conversation instead of avoiding people during lunch time, and practicing a few minutes of meditation in the morning instead of hitting the snooze button several times.

One method that is commonly used to help keep a person motivated while changing habits is to keep a calendar somewhere prominent in your home. Alternatively, you can use an app on your phone. The idea is that you have somewhere to mark each day that you successfully complete your new habit or avoid your bad one. A person will take anywhere from a couple of weeks to several months to break a habit or form a new habit, so don't worry if it is taking a little longer than you expected. It doesn't mean you are less capable; each person simply has a unique pathway toward learning.

Once you have your plan in place, prioritize your one simple change each day. No step forward is too small. If you find that exercising every single day after work is not something you can do, redesign your daily habit to something that you feel confident you can accomplish each day. Focus on just 15 to 20 minutes of exercise a day, at whatever time is convenient. It may be difficult to stick to the same exact time every day, so personalize your task so that you are giving yourself the best possible chance of success. Each day, make a point to acknowledge your accomplishment by checking off that day on the calendar or in your app. This is important, as it gives us a feeling of accomplishment and offers a big of a boost to keep the routine going.

Once you have a bit of a streak going, you will find it easier to continue along with the momentum you've got going. Human beings are hardwired to be somewhat more loss averse in comparison to desiring a gain of some kind.

For example, as data has shown in various research studies, people tend to fear losing 5 dollars much more strongly than they desire to go after an additional 5 dollars. That idea of loss simply carries more weight. This principle will help you as you begin to see the checkmarks adding up across your calendar. At some point, you will start to feel more and more strongly about not breaking the streak you have going. It feels good to know that you are capable of this daily change. And within no time, you will have formed a new healthy daily habit.

Positive Reinforcement

You are probably familiar with the concept of positive reinforcement, even if you can't perfectly explain it. Ever heard of Pavlov's dog?

Pavlov's dog refers to an experiment that was conducted by Ivan Pavlov where he successfully trained a dog to associate the smell of food, which made the dog salivate, with other stimuli which would not usually make a dog salivate, like the sound of a bell. Before long, the dog would salivate at the sound of a bell, even if there was no actual food around. This is one of the most famous examples of what is now known as associative learning.

The dog goes through a series of conditioning that ultimately leads it to associate salivation with a neutral sound.

When we introduce positive reinforcement into the picture, there is another dimension to the learning process that involves a reward system. Positive reinforcement is simply when a specific behavior is rewarded with something desirable. For example, you might tell a child that if he behaves while he's out with mom running errands, then they will stop and get some ice cream on the way home. This reward, and anticipation of a reward, motivates the child to behave while he is out doing boring things with mom. Positive reinforcement works to support learning only when the reward system is consistent. Another example of positive reinforcement is the little shiny stickers teachers might put on a child's homework assignment to tell the child he did a good job. Each time the child turns in a homework assignment, the assignment is returned to him with one of these stickers. The sticker is a symbol that says the teacher is proud of the work the child has done. Children like to impress their parents and teachers, so this often serves as a powerful source of positive reinforcement.

This idea can be applied to your own life as you discipline yourself to follow your daily habit regimen. It may be enough for you to look way down the road and be able to see yourself having successfully formed your new habit, but some of you will find that you need an extra boost of motivation every now and then to keep going. It makes sense that this happens.

Sometimes, the reward for realizing a positive new habit doesn't come for a long time, even if you know it will be very beneficial over the long term. Human beings tend to be drawn toward instant gratification, and this is encouraged by services that deliver exactly what you want either immediately or within a short amount of time. Just about anything you may want is available online and can be shipped to you within a single day, if you choose to pay for it. A hundred different delivery services will go get the food you're craving and deliver it to you within a half hour. If we want to see a new movie or TV show, all we have to do is get online to our favorite streaming services.

Our society has evolved to encourage instant gratification, and, as a result, a lot of us tend to struggle with the idea of working for the long-term and patience in getting what we want. You've seen the ads and commercials depicting a woman who fails on her diet because she is too tempted by junk food or sugar. She may really want to lose weight, but the lure of sugar is too much for her to overcome.

Because of this phenomenon, it may become necessary to introduce a system of positive reinforcement as you are in the fragile beginning stages of forming new habits. This means that you will reward yourself for the fact that you've kept up with your daily goals periodically throughout your journey. It could be every week or every couple of weeks, maybe something a little bigger once a month. As always, getting out that journal and writing out some ideas will help you come up with a plan that will motivate you.

Think of something that you really enjoy and that would be a powerful motivator for you to accomplish your goals. Perhaps once a week you will treat yourself to some of your favorite ice cream or let yourself buy some clothing or a pair of shoes. Maybe if you can complete two weeks of following your daily tasks, you treat yourself to a pair of tickets to a sports game you'd really like to see. Whatever motivates you and excites you, use it as a way to keep yourself going during those times when the daily task feels more like a chore.

I promise you will feel this on occasion, and it is perfectly normal.

Another tool that I come back to again and again is simply setting aside time every single day to write about what you are experiencing. Many times, our feelings are not very clear, and taking time to write and flesh out the origins of our emotions can go a long way in helping us address the source of those emotions.

If you are feeling tired, or perhaps you miss a day of your habit-forming task, write down in your journal why you think you felt that way or lapsed on your daily task. Is there something else in your life that is bothering you or causing anxiety? Perhaps there is a distraction that needs to be dealt with. This is why I spend so much time emphasizing the importance of rooting out negative influences, both internal and external, before embarking on this habit-forming journey. But sometimes there will be things outside your control that you have to deal with before moving forward, and that's okay. Take some time to address what is holding you back, just like we focused on doing in previous chapters, then take some time to regroup before trying again. Remember, failure is an inevitable part of success, and there will be obstacles to overcome as you work toward your goals. Give yourself as much support as possible by doing your best to remove sources of anxiety and stress from your life before introducing new habits.

As you regroup, write about how you are feeling. Perhaps you don't know exactly what led you off track. Go back as far as you can as you recall your progress to pinpoint exactly where things went wrong.

If you are simply dealing with a lack of motivation, try writing about how far you've come and what it will mean to you when you achieve your goals. Return to that visualization of yourself having accomplished your goals as often as possible and as often as you need; that's why it's there. If you can keep this visualization in your sights at all times, especially when things start getting difficult, you will be giving yourself extra support and motivation to get through the rough spots.

Another source of support may be available to you through trusted family, friends, or romantic partner. Set up a time to meet and talk over coffee or something and explain what you are trying to do. Be open and let your feelings out about whatever doubts you have about whether or not you will accomplish your goals. Feeling doubt is not a failure on your part, it is natural. Also, feeling self-doubt is a strong sign that what you are doing is important to you, because you are invested in the outcome and realize what is at stake. Keep reminding yourself of the reward to come.

When you combine all of these strategies for support, you will find that you have a much stronger foundation from which to move forward. Keep journaling, ask for help or just talk with friends and family, integrate a system of periodic positive reinforcement, and keep your personal vision handy at all times to combat thought of self-doubt that come up. People are usually stronger than they think in the moment. Arm yourself to be as strong and as likely to succeed as possible.

Negative Reinforcement

Negative reinforcement is often misunderstood as the equivalent to punishment, but this is incorrect.

Negative reinforcement refers to the taking away of a stimulus, the act of which encourages a specific behavior. A good example is the little beeping alarm that goes off in your car when you don't have your seatbelt. This is a form of negative reinforcement because you are encouraged to buckle your seatbelt because you want the annoying beeping sound to go away. It is the counterpart of positive reinforcement in that it also encourages a certain behavior, but instead of adding a positive reinforcer, you are simply getting rid of a negatively impactful stimulus. Punishment, on the other hand, is the use of a negative consequence of a certain behavior. You steal from a store, you go to jail as punishment. This is very different from negative reinforcement.

Negative reinforcement can also work for you in terms of strengthening your resolve to keep going with your daily habit-forming tasks. To use the example of quitting smoking again, you will very quickly begin to see the physical benefits of taking away the cigarette smoking. You are rewarded, through negative reinforcement with an improvement in overall wellbeing, energy, food tasting better, breathing easier, etc. The list of benefits is extensive in this example. If the idea of negative reinforcement applies in your personal situation, take some time each day or every couple of days to take note of the benefits you are receiving as you remove that negative thing from your life. Write regularly and keep going back to those pages each time you feel challenged to keep going.

Moving Forward

You should be proud of yourself for beginning this life-changing journey! You now have the essential tools you will need to be successful. Revisit these chapters as you make progress and remember to share your success with others for additional support. There is nothing better than receiving a hug or acknowledgement of your work from those you love and trust.

In chapters 9 and 10, you will learn how to introduce additional tools into your new life practice, including meditation and a list of 10 daily practices to strengthen self-confidence.

Chapter 9: Meditation Techniques

Meditation has become one of the most popular self-help techniques to ever reach the Western world. There are countless books available offering extensive history and instruction for newcomers who would like to learn what meditation is all about.

In this chapter, I will give you a general introduction to the practice of meditation, why it is useful, and how you can begin introducing it into your daily life as a way to strengthen your goal of forming new habits.

Why Meditation?

The practice of meditation has been around for a very, very, very long time. Until fairly recently, meditation was usually tied in most people's mind to a certain religion of spiritual practice. There was always a whole history and spiritual tradition behind the actual practice. The most familiar example of this is Buddhism.

Buddhism is nearly synonymous with meditation in a lot of people's minds. The story of the "first" Buddha and his enlightenment is taught as the first stepping stone toward realizing each person's inner "Buddha nature" within themselves. Consistent meditation practice over a period of time is how people get to this idea of enlightenment, though the syntax for believers assures that there is no journey toward, but simply a realization.

Meditation became mainstream in the Western world, and soon there were lots of different sects and groups of people trying to popularize their own group's meditation "style." One of the most well known might be the Transcendental Meditation movement, popularized by such figures as David Lynch and Gwyneth Paltrow.

The fact is, meditation is available for anyone and everyone to learn and practice. Some people will latch on to certain styles and spiritual practices and belief systems associated with it, but this is not necessary. You do not have to be religious or adhere to any set of spiritual beliefs to benefit from a daily mediations practice, and that's because the effects of meditation are scientifically documented and well-researched.

Something very profound happens in the brain during a deep meditation. During meditation, the practitioner is essentially cleansing and repairing the brain similar to the process that occurs during a deep sleep. Similar to the benefits of sleep, meditation encourages the organization and solidification of information necessary for long-term learning and muscle memory.

For example, perhaps you yourself or someone you knew in childhood trained in a musical instrument, either for school or personal enjoyment. You would study and practice with a teacher for an hour or two, then at the end you kind of felt overwhelmed with information and things you needed to practice.

You may have found that after a good night's rest, you would wake up and feel refreshed with a better organization of information in your mind. The next time you sat down to play, it seemed easier and more clear to get out the notes and play a piece that you may have been struggling with just a day or two previously.

This is the brain hard at work for you as it works to make the pathways and neural connections as streamlined as possible. Meditation has the same effect when it is practiced consistently over time.

This is why meditation would be an excellent tool for you to introduce into your daily life as your brain works to form new habits. It doesn't have to be a long meditation; just 20 minutes a day will go a long way. We talked about mindfulness earlier in this book, and you can easily adapt this principle of mindfulness into a concentrated 20-

minute daily meditation through a variety of techniques.

Mindfulness Meditation

When we discussed mindfulness, you learned about the practice of reining in your thoughts to focus on the "here and now" as opposed to all of the other things fighting for space in your mind. You practiced focusing your thoughts and focusing on what is going on right before you instead of something that happened last week or your to-do list for the next day or the next week. It is not easy to adopt this practice at first, especially for a complete beginner. But there is nothing better for your brain as you begin training it to change and form better, healthier habits.

In this section, I will walk you through a basic meditation that you can begin implementing into your life immediately. You don't need to pay for special instruction or study a thousand years of history to understand and experience the power of meditation.

First, you will need to find a space inside your home that is comfortable and free of distraction. This may be more challenging for those of you who live in apartments with roommates or a similar situation but try to find a space either inside your home or, if the weather permits, someplace outside that is quiet. I wouldn't suggest going out to a public park or a similar setting for your first few sessions as the background noise might be quite distracting.

Once you've found a quiet spot, assume a comfortable position. You don't have to twist your body or legs into complex positions like you've seen people do in movies or advertisements. Sit however is comfortable for you. If you decide you want to get more serious about meditation in the future, there is a ton of information and history waiting for you to discover in order to learn more complex techniques, such as Zazen according the Zen Buddhist tradition. For now, your goal is simply to remove any stress and tension from your body so that you can completely focus on what's going on inside your mind.

To begin releasing this tension, we will start with something called a "body scan." Bringing your awareness to the present moment entails that you are also as aware as possible of your own body in space. It may sound weird, but we actually go through most of our day-to-day lives without consciously feeling many areas of our bodies. Our brains simply choose to bypass this awareness in favor of a task at work or whatever else our daily routines demand of us.

To start with a body scan, first bring your attention to your toes and feet. Move them slowly to help you with this, then begin taking slow, deep breaths. Thinking about your feet, slowly begin to relax and release as much tension as possible from your feet. It may help to first tense the muscles, then slowly relax the muscles. Visualize the tension floating away on the air.

Next, move your focus to your ankles, your calves, the rest of your legs. Gradually focus on each part and slowly relax as far as possible. You may find that the best position for this exercise is lying flat on your back to help you relax.

At the halfway point, take a few minutes to focus on your breathing. Don't worry if you have trouble focusing. Your mind is going to want to wander on different things, and that's okay. Don't try to force your mind blank. Instead, when you realize your thoughts are wandering away, simply restore your focus on the task at hand whenever you realize what's happening. Try not to get frustrated with yourself if it is hard to focus at first. Meditation is not something that comes natural to everyone, and as we all continue through our lives in an information overload society, it makes sense that the brain has trouble calming down. Simply redirect your thoughts and come back to the present moment. Focusing on your breathing is one of the simplest tools you can use for practicing mindfulness and throughout your dedicated meditation sessions.

Now, move the focus up to your torso. Put your hand just under your ribcage and feel the breaths you are taking as they come from deep within, then release. Do this several times, feeling the breath as you inhale, then slowly releasing. As you exhale, focus on relaxing and releasing as much tension as possible.

Finally, move the focus throughout your arms, then move up to your head. The last point is the very top of your head. Hold this focus for several breaths, then release.

Congratulations! You've just completed your first meditation. If you are brand new to the practice, I would suggest trying to fit in just a few minutes of meditation every day while you practice your new habits, but don't overwhelm yourself by trying to adopt a 20-minute meditation routine right away. If it works for your set of habits, it might be beneficial to try and schedule your daily habitual task alongside a meditation session. Keep track of how you feel and write down notes to keep track. How do you feel directly following a meditation session? Is it something you feel you can benefit from on a daily basis? Keep in mind that you may be able to find a nearby group or meetup that practices meditation. Having a mentor and teacher to help you develop your practice is the ideal way to get better and maintain a daily meditation practice. If the group meets weekly for meditation, consider incorporating this into your habit-forming task list. As you use meditation to clear you mind and focus, your dedication and ability to maintain your daily habit-forming task streak will become stronger and stronger.

Guided Meditation 2: Mantra

A mantra is simply a script that you use as the focus of your meditation session. There are thousands of different mantras and scripts, and you can also choose to create your own. You may have heard of the practice called "loving-kindness" meditation. This meditation entails focusing on an outward radiation of love and kindness towards the world through scripts that reinforce this feeling of love and oneness. A simple Google search will provide you with tons of examples of scripts to use for this mantra meditation. We've actually mentioned one already in the chapter where we used Laura and her daily task of reciting words of self-confidence each morning. Again, you can choose from a list of others' scripts or create your own. The idea is to choose something that is central to what you are trying to cultivate in your heart and within your mind.

Find your comfortable spot in the house or outside if the weather is nice and there are not too many distractions. Relax your body and settle in to a comfortable position. Take a few deep breaths to help you relax. Observe your thoughts as they wander but don't force your mind to go blank or push thoughts away. Let the thoughts happen, then gently redirect back to your breath and present space. Begin by visualizing yourself in front of you, the stresses of your day weighing heavily on your back.

Visualize these as stress that is captured inside a helium balloon. Focus in on each one. Maybe you had a difficult customer you had to deal with that day, or you had an argument with a coworker. Maybe you feel nervous about an upcoming bill, or you have an obligation coming up that you are not looking forward to. Whatever the source of stress, you are going to gently let go of each one through a visualization exercise.

Concentrate on one stress at a time, then visualize your hand on the string of the balloon as you let go and the balloon begins to rise. Watch in your mind's eye as the stress begins to float away from you, higher and higher into the sky. As you watch, the balloon gets smaller and smaller until you can barely see it, then it disappears. Do this for each of the triggers for stress that your mind keeps moving toward. After you've released the last balloon, take a deep breath alongside the picture of yourself in your mind. Now, recite your mantra.

Either write down or memorize your chosen mantra and begin saying the words slowly aloud. Really focus in on the words and what they mean to you. Let them build you up like you are putting on a suit of armor. Feel the conviction in your voice and internalize the words. Reinforce the mantra by repeating aloud the words, then silently contemplate their meaning. Continue to visualize yourself embodying the attitude of the words in your mantra. If you are concentrating on a loving-kindness mantra, imagine yourself surrounded by others with whom you are sharing warm smiles and hugs. If you are focusing on your own inner strength, imagine yourself performing a daily ritual with the conviction of strength and confidence you want to maintain. Whatever the words of your mantra lead you toward, imagine yourself in a position of strength in conjunction with those words. The mind will internalize this feeling of empowerment, and you will be able to call on this energy when you need it.

Basics of Zazen

Some meditation practices call for the practitioner to try to focus hard on a mantra or other point of focus. Other meditations want you to try to erase your thoughts and quiet your mind through conscious effort.

Zazen, or "seated meditation," is an ancient meditation practice that is tied in with Zen Buddhist philosophy and teaching. I want to briefly introduce this tradition, as many people find it to be one of the most transformational and wonderful experiences of their lives to utilize this meditation daily.

Formal Zen meditation calls for a certain posture and body position, but you don't have to try tackling all of the details at once. This meditation is all about watching your thoughts as they move without hindering their movement. It is different in that you are not trying to exercise control, but instead go with the flow according to the principle of impermanence. A thought will land on a certain thing, it may linger a bit, then is moves along. There is no standing in place or freezing the mind on one subject because that is not the natural order of things.

To experience what I mean, go ahead and assume your comfortable position and begin simply watching your thought patterns. We've touched a bit on this during our focus on mindfulness, but instead of trying to reign in your thoughts and redirecting, simply try not to dwell on any one thought for longer than a few moments. Watch the movement as the thoughts come and go and where they tend to linger a little before moving on. Do you keep coming back to some stressful recent experience? Perhaps your mind wanders into territory where you begin to feel anxious about possibilities. As soon as this thought enters your mind, try to gently brush it along as you move on to a different thought. The idea is to not get "stuck" on any one thought and to watch the continuous movement through your mind.

In "proper" Zazen practice, the practitioner will sit up straight, perhaps with the help of a small cushion, with his head gently relaxed and slightly tilted forward. The eyes are slightly open and are directed at the ground just in front of him. Arms rest in his lap with one hand resting in the other, the thumbs forming a small "O" in the center. The added discipline for forma meditation adds a whole new dimension to the experience and should be reserved for when you become more practiced. The most important part is getting started and getting your mind used to the jolt of redirection and focus.

Whatever style you choose to pursue, I highly recommend that you choose one to incorporate into your daily routine. Meditation can be a powerful and rejuvenating way to start your day if you can set aside just 20 minutes before heading out the door for work or whatever daily tasks you have planned. Even if you are simply setting aside a few minutes to practice mindfulness, bringing your attention to the present, this is going to form a powerful source of strength and motivation for you as you build better habits.

Give yourself time to master techniques such as the ones mentioned in this chapter. It is a skill, just as learning to rewire your brain is. Trust your capacity and ability to form new habits through simple repetition and conviction. Believe in what you are doing and where it will lead you.

In our final chapter, we will go through a list of 10 useful daily practices that you can incorporate into your routine to support self-confidence. A breakdown in self-confidence can be a big blow to your ability to keep moving forward. Reinforce your determination with these tips to keep you going, even on those challenging days when you need extra motivation. As always, never lose sight of your personal goal visualization, standing in that victory pose with a giant smile on your face!

Chapter 10: Moving Forward: 10 Daily Practices to Strengthen Self-Confidence

Building self-confidence is essential to maintaining the attitude and the energy to persevere in your journey towards a better life through better habits. As you check off those days and watch the chain grow across your calendar, there are several things you can do to help you stay motivated. Integrating a daily meditation practice is an excellent way to help your brain as it is challenged to rewire itself towards a better state.

In addition, I'd like to offer the following 10 daily practices for building self-confidence. All of them are simple and easy-to-use tools to help you stay focused and your mind to stay on track.

Daily Practice #1: Compliment a Stranger

Your first daily practice tip is all about going out of your way to compliment a stranger. If you are a shy person, then this may be a little more challenging to you than to someone who is naturally outgoing, but the benefits of accomplishing this daily task will be powerful for anyone who undertakes it.

You don't have to overthink this practice. Simply go about your day but be conscious of the people around you. Not only will you be more mindful of how you can help those around you, but this also allows you to incorporate a valuable practice of mindfulness into your day. For example, say you are at the grocery store and you are waiting in line with several other people. Instead of blankly staring at the gum, think of something nice to say to the person either in front of you or behind you. It may be something as simple as complimenting a piece of clothing or jewelry. Or perhaps you want to tell them they have a beautiful smile. I promise you that just a simple gesture like this one can light up a person's whole day.

Think of a time when this happened to you. It meant a lot, didn't it? It seems like such a simple gesture, but there is a profound power in human connection, even in something as simple as a compliment. You may find that you love the feeling so much, you start practicing complimenting strangers automatically. The key is to stay mindful of what's going on around you. Everything in that grocery store or in your workplace or school has a special set of circumstances affecting their lives. Many of them are struggling with something challenging, so taking the time to say something nice to someone can have a much larger impact than even you can imagine in the moment.

Daily Practice #2: Lift Weight

Now, don't panic! Let's look a little deeper into this tip.

We talked a little bit about getting more exercise every day and how it isn't necessary to do a monster workout every single day to improve your health. This is still the truth, and there are lots of options for you to choose from that will only take a few minutes out of your day. It will be well worth it.

Consider investing in a pair of dumbbells. They are not expensive, and you can tailor the weight according to what you are comfortable with. You can get hand weights as light as 3 lbs. all the way up to 40 lbs. and higher. Lifting weights for just a few minutes a day is going to benefit you in many different ways.

First of all, it's obviously good for muscle toning, and you also get the benefits of those feel good chemicals we discussed early on in the book in relation to emotions. The chemicals released into your body as a result of exercise is a natural high that boosts your mood, as well as your self-esteem. Lifting weight gives you a feeling of accomplishment that is immediate and long-lasting. You will continue to feel good for a long time after challenging yourself with some weights.

And you don't necessarily need hand weights to get the benefits of this type of exercise. There are several different exercises you can do which challenge you using your own body weight. Some examples include: pushups, plank, burpees, lunges, and squats. You will find plenty of resources online to show you how to properly execute each of these exercises. They don't take up much room, and a simple 10 to 20-minute workout is all you need to focus on to begin adding this daily practice into your routine.

The confidence streams naturally from having accomplished a weight-lifting feat. You may find that you love the feeling so much, you want to gradually add weight to add to the challenge, and that's great! Be careful not to challenge yourself too far in the beginning, especially if these exercises are new to you. Remember, try to do a little bit even if you don't feel like it. The simple action of beginning the workout will give your energy a boost even if you were convinced you had nothing in you that day.

Daily Practice #3: Watch a Motivational or Inspiring Video/Presentation

This is one of my favorite practices. It requires very little effort on your part and in return, you receive a boost in mood as well as self-confidence.

We human beings favor storytelling when it comes to passing on lessons, from fairy tales and fables teaching us valuable ethical behavior to historical study that tells us all about our triumphs and failures as a species. Taking time each day for a motivational video or even just to sit down and read some motivational quotes by famous speakers will help raise your self-confidence and also get you excited about moving forward to new challenges. There is nothing better than a good speech or talk. Head to YouTube or Google a favorite figure to see if you can find just what you are looking for. There are so many things to choose from. TED Talks are plentiful and easy to find on YouTube. There are TED Talks that are free to view on YouTube that cover an endless list of topics from a variety of speakers from all over the world. Choose a topic that you are personally interested, or else find a talk which directly addresses topics like confidence, conquering your fears, and forming good habits. There is a great deal for you to discover, and it just takes a few minutes to reap the reward of a good old-fashioned pep talk.

This daily practice is especially helpful on days when you feel less motivated than usual. You may feel like you have less energy and are just not on top of things the way you usually are. I promise, after a few minutes of listening to a motivational speech from a respected figure, you will feel renewed and imbued with a fresh surge of energy and positivity. The feeling is contagious, and when someone speaks from the heart with the intent of spreading it to listeners, it is impossible not to pick up on that energy. Use it to keep you going throughout the rest of your day.

Daily Practice #4: Learn Something New

The brain needs regular exercise just like the body does. This daily practice is all about using your brain power to improve your cognitive function, memory, and learning. It may sound like a lot to take on, certainly for a daily practice, so I'm going to suggest a plan of action to get you started with this.

The idea is to engage your brain in a new skill. It doesn't have to be super challenging or overwhelming. Unless you are really motivated and interested in doing so, I wouldn't suggest buying a college textbook on chemistry, for example, and trying to teach yourself all of the lessons. Learning something new can be as simple as reading an article on a new piece of technology in the newspaper. Perhaps you have a special interest in something like planes, or historical war tactics, or psychology, or flight patterns of birds. Whatever sounds interesting to you, look up a short article that will teach you something new about that topic. I would suggest making sure to check the sources for the articles you read, as some are going to be of better quality and more researched than others. This new knowledge will make you feel stimulated and will wake up your brain, helping you to focus on other tasks. It is too easy nowadays to simply let your mind melt while you take in hundreds of images and mindless text from social media and other apps on your phone. Be proactive with your brain's development and feed it something with a little more meat on it! You brain will thank you. It feels a lot like finishing a meditation session. Concentrating on a scholarly text helps to flush away needless background information as you bring all of your faculties to focus on the words you are reading.

Alternatively, perhaps there is a skill you've always wanted to learn but have never had time for. Set aside some time each day to practice learning a new skill that you will enjoy. It shouldn't feel like a big chore, because if it does, you will find it very difficult to continue practicing. Perhaps you've always wanted to learn to juggle! Find some instruction online and watch some videos to show you how you can get started, then practice for a few minutes each day. You will be surprised at how much better you feel emotionally and mentally as a result of exercising your brain in this way.

Daily Practice #5: Power Pose and Posture

Okay, so this daily practice should sound familiar, and it should be an easy daily practice to incorporate into your schedule. While the initial exercise doesn't last long, you will benefit a great deal from trying to maintain the posture and forming a habit of holding yourself in a way that boosts your confidence automatically. Let's review and try it.

Stand with your back straight and your shoulders back. Hold your chin parallel with the floor. Take it a bit further by putting a smile on your face. You will feel the difference, trust me!

Now, raise your arms above your head to form a V. Form fists with your hands, just like you see an athlete doing when he scores a touchdown or makes a basket in basketball. Hold your arms straight and maintain your posture. While you hold this pose, reflect on how this makes you feel. How did your mood change in just the last few seconds? Do you feel any different? How is your confidence level?

Instead of dismissing this exercise right away, challenge yourself to think about your posture as you go about your day. See how it make you feel and whether or not it alters your mood in any way. Most of all, see how it affects your confidence. You don't have to raise your arms up in a victory pose at work, but I highly recommend keeping some kind of reminder at your desk to help you remember to sit up straight and tall. This is not only much better for your back, but it's been shown to help confidence level as well as productivity. It is easier to feel in control and top of a heavy workload when your body exudes confidence. As your body reflects a position of confidence, it will infiltrate your mind until your attitude reflects the same confidence.

You can practice smiling as a way to improve your mood as well. Make it your goal to offer people smiles as you walk by them. You will most likely receive a warm smile in return, and it may even prompt a pleasant conversation, opening up possibilities for connection that may not have existed before.

Daily Practice #6: Practice Failure

This one might sound a little odd to you. What do I mean by practice failure? Wouldn't this just make you better at...failing? The answer is, surprisingly, no. And I will explain why.

Failure is an inevitable part of life. We fail a few times when we first learn to walk, to ride a bike, or climb a tree. We fail a few times when we first start trying to talk to individuals we're interested in dating, and we fail on first dates…at least, a lot of us do.

We need to prepare ourselves for the inevitable failure that comes with trying something new and challenging. It's when we are unprepared for how to handle failure that we crash and burn. Preparing yourself for what it might feel like to fail at a certain task will make the actual experience less devastating. When we set up expectations that are too high or too demanding, we set ourselves up for catastrophic failure. For example, if you had pressured yourself to adopt one new habit every single week without thinking about what this entails and how it might not be possible, you might have been devastated at the end of that first week, leading to frustration and perhaps even giving up on trying again. We've got to get to know ourselves as well as our limits. Get to know not only your strengths, but your weaknesses. Form a plan for a couple of different ways to approach a problem should you find that the first way is not the best. This will make you smarter and more ready for whatever comes around the corner.

You don't have to necessarily fail every single day as a way to practice failure, but a good daily practice is to wrap your mind around the possibility of failure, even in the simplest of tasks, then walk yourself through how it wouldn't be a big deal because you can always try again. Get your brain used to the possibility, and it won't so much of a surprise when those failures come around. Put a positive spin on failure by looking at it this way: You've found one more way *not* to do something! You can now avoid making the same mistakes in the future.

Daily Practice #7: Transform Your Morning

This daily practice will look different for each person depending on how their days are set up, but there are some general guidelines you can follow to optimize your morning for productivity, confidence and attitude throughout the rest of your day.

Does your current morning routine look something like this?—You hit the snooze once, twice…maybe three times. You roll out of bed, throw on some clothes, and head to the bathroom to brush your teeth as you think about how much you don't want to go to work that day. After brushing your teeth, you fix your hair for a second or two then fill a travel mug full of coffee before rushing out the door, just barely on track to get to work on time. Sound familiar?

If it does, I'm sure you're aware that this might not be the most ideal way to start your day. Our attitudes and moods at the very beginning of a day has a powerful influence on how the rest of our days are going to go. If we wake up in a bad mood, just sure that it's going to be a bad day…odds are, that's exactly how it's going to turn out. This happens because of the principle that we "see what we want to see." If we start out the day with a pessimistic attitude, we are going to go through our days seeing only the bad and the unlucky moments. But the truth is that this doesn't have to be our reality. We do have a choice…and it begins with redesigning your morning.

If you don't have much time in the morning and it stresses you out, then your first challenge is going to be to simply make more time for yourself in the morning by going to bed earlier and setting your alarm to go off a little earlier. A half hour is all you need, but you'll have to really put in the effort at first to change up your routine. Your body is going to scream at you to just lay there for another 30 minutes like usual, but I promise you, once you start to adopt this new morning ritual, you won't want to go back.

The idea is to set aside enough time for you to comfortably wake, have some kind of breakfast, then sit down for some personal "quiet time." The only requirement for quiet time is that you aren't online browsing the internet or any media sites. Take this time to read for a few minutes, start a new book you've been meaning to. Or, you could use this time to get in a mindfulness meditation session or practice that new skill you've decided to learn. Whatever it is, the idea is that it will put you in a calm, peaceful place before the chaos of the day takes over. Just a few minutes a day like this in the morning will make a big difference in your overall attitude, alertness, and confidence. And it won't take long to see this effect in action. Don't take my word for it. Try it!

Daily Practice #8: Pamper Yourself Once in a While

You may not have time every single day to do something extravagant, like a day at the spa or a new haircut or shopping spree, but you can take a few minutes each day to remind yourself of your reward as you earn it by conquering your daily habit-forming tasks.

Decide what you love best when it comes to pampering. We talked earlier about the power of positive reinforcement. You will be using the same concept here. Plan a day that will be all about you, when you can take it easy and relax, maybe treat yourself to a good meal at one of your favorite restaurants or take your partner out for a fun date night. Whatever you plan to do, make it a reality by setting down a hard plan and sticking to it once it comes around. Don't talk yourself out of it when the time comes with excuses like, Gee, I should save the money, or, I don't know if I worked hard enough for this. Don't let these discouraging voices keep you from rewarding yourself. Remember, you don't have be ready for the marathon after your first day of training. It takes consistent practice and dedication to accomplish your life goals. Treating yourself will give you something concrete and short-term to look forward to, and you'll be looking forward to the next treat as soon as you're done!

Daily Practice #9: Sleep!

This may seem like an obvious one, but you may be shocked at how many people do not get nearly enough sleep each night. When we don't get enough sleep, the body has to function on something called a sleep deficit, which is never made up for until we get that sleep that the body needs.

Many vitally important things happen when we sleep, and it is especially important for our brains. Set aside time to give yourself a solid 8 hours of sleep each and every night.

Daily Practice #10: Write

You knew this was coming. Keep up with the journaling! There is nothing more motivating than being able to look back and review your progress. See how far you've come and take notes on how your progress makes you feel. Just reading about past victories will automatically boost your confidence and keep you going for the rest of the day.

Conclusion

Conquering your bad habits through mind hacking to make way for new ones is one of the most important and life-changing endeavors a human being can pursue. From the time we are very young, we are programmed to feel and think a certain way until a point at which we begin to think for ourselves. Friends, family and authority figures can have a large impact on how we think and on the habits we cultivate, and these habits may continue for the rest of our lives.

When we begin to think and experience life on our own, we inevitably pick up some not-so-good habits along the way. These habits tend to develop slowly over time so that we do not even know they are a problem until they seem out of control. But these don't have to out of your control. Through the tips and strategies you've learned about in this book, you have the tools necessary to begin addressing these bad habits one by one before building up new, healthier habits in their place. These new habits are personal to you, and you should never feel pressured to adopt another's lifestyle out of obligation or pressure. Only you know what truly makes you happy and what you truly want out of life, and no one can take that from you.

You've learned the foundation of what mind hacking is all about as well as how our emotions can sometimes have a big impact on our behaviors. Because the feeling brain is quicker than the thinking brain, it can be easy to let yourself lose control and let emotions take the wheel in your mind. But the good news is that it doesn't have to be that way. You can exercise control over your emotions and behaviors through a proactive approach to thought.

After learning how emotion translates into behavior through some of the most outrageous and fascinating social experiments ever conducted, you were introduced to the principles of neuroplasticity. Neuroplasticity is what makes it possible for you to change your brain and redesign what you want your life to look like through cultivating new, better habits.

Even the most powerful emotions can be addressed through a consistent routine of mind-altering practices. You learned all about some of the most negative and hindering emotions a person can feel, including anxiety, worry and overthinking. You also learned how you can take control of these emotions by redirecting your negative thought trajectories toward a more positive pattern of thought.

Step 1 in the mind hacking process took you through the difficult process of identifying those negative outward influences which may be holding you back. After identifying and removing these negative influences from your life, you were ready to move forward to step 2.

Step 2 walked you through how to vividly portray your personal life goals through the practice of visualization. After creating a clear picture in your mind of where you were going, it was time to start taking your first steps.

Step 3 in the mind hacking process was all about setting small goals and taking small, manageable steps to gradually realize your goals. To keep you going throughout this process, you learned the fundamentals of meditation and how you can use this practice to strengthen your resolve to keep moving forward.

Finally, we introduced 10 effective daily practices to help you cultivate a sense of strength and self-confidence. As you continue on in your journey, remember to periodically reflect on your accomplishments and consider sharing your journey with others so that they might also have the opportunity to mind hack their way to success and happiness.